LUNATIC
A Practical Guide to the Moon and Back

LUNATIC

(**A Practical Guide to the Moon and Back**)

Katrin Swartenbroux
Wided Bouchrika

𝕃 | LANNOO

I am one
with the ebb and flow,
that's all I know

BROCKHAMPTON
Sweet

(

IDENTIKIT OF THE MOON

(

MOON-GAZING THROUGHOUT THE CENTURIES

How the moon changed in significance and meaning
throughout history

AT FIRST GLANCE

The moon as a magical celestial body and calendar

THE RACE FOR SPACE

The moon as a scientific and political object

NEED FOR MYSTICISM

The moon as a tool for self-care and connection with nature

THE MOON OF TOMORROW

The moon as a tourist destination and economic resource

(

THE MOON AS A MUSE

The moon as a source of inspiration for artists,
musicians and writers

THE MOON IN WRITING

THE MOON IN PAINTING

THE MOON IN SONG

(

THE POWER OF THE MOON

How the moon influences life on Earth

97

MOONLIGHT

105

THE TIDES

109

MAGNETIC FIELD

115

(

USE THE MOON

Discover how you can use the moon in your daily life

119

LUNAR CYCLES

How do you make the most of the different lunar phases?

121

OTHER MOON PHENOMENA

What is a blue moon, a blood moon
and a super moon?

132

MOON RITUALS

From moon-bathing to smudging

136

MOON-GAZING FOR BEGINNERS

What, where and when is the best way of looking at the moon?

142

MOON HOROSCOPE

Calculate your moon sign and learn what that means

157

(

ADDENDA

175

IDENTIKIT OF THE MOON

WHAT

The moon is the only natural satellite orbiting the Earth,
and one of the five biggest moons in our solar system.

HOW

The moon revolves around the Earth in 27.3217 days .

DISTANCE TO EARTH

between 357,000 km and 406,000 km

AGE

approximately 4.53 billion years old

CIRCUMFERENCE

10,916 km

DIAMETER

3476 km

MASS

7.35×10^{22} kg

MOON-GAZING THROUGHOUT THE CENTURIES

HOW THE MOON CHANGED IN SIGNIFICANCE AND MEANING THROUGHOUT HISTORY

The moon has always enchanted us. As a muse, as a possible deity, as a convenient calendar, as a magical celestial body, as a destination that determines power or as a money maker: our fascination with the moon has been inspired for various reasons across the centuries.

Selene, the Greek goddess of the moon

AT FIRST GLANCE
The moon as a magical celestial body and calendar

As long as we can remember, the night has always been accompanied by a presence outlined in the inky sky. Sometimes crescent-shaped, sometimes a perfect disc, occasionally no more than a dim shadow of itself. It is not hard to imagine that special powers were attributed to this enigmatic phenomenon.

In various civilisations, the moon was depicted as a deity and a supernatural phenomenon, a subject of mythology and folklore.

The moon was seen as the counterpart of the sun, much like night is the opposite of day. In Greek and Roman culture, the sun and moon were depicted as male (Helios/Sol) and female (Selene/Luna). The Chinese saw the moon as the chill *yin* to balance the fiery *yang* of the sun. In part due to the monthly cycle of the moon, the satellite was also associated with the menstrual cycle and therefore with all that was feminine. However, not all lunar deities from all civilisations and cultures have been female. The Egyptians had various male moon gods, including Ibis, Set, Thoth and Khonsu; the Mesopotamians had Sin, while the Inuit visualised the moon through Igaluk.

The moon also played an important role in the development of astrology. Even in ancient Babylon, the observations of celestial bodies led to records of omens that predicted events about the land, the harvest and the fate of kings. Astrology continued to develop throughout the Middle Ages, and the moon was also used in occult practices: witches were alleged to use the different phases of the moon to power their magic.

The moon is also used as the basis for our calendars. The different phases of the moon – half-moon, full moon, crescent moon – were used to mark the passage of time. Archaeologists have found sticks and bones dating back as far as twenty to thirty thousand years ago that have different lines carved into them, which are believed to represent the different phases of the moon. Our thirty-day month is an approximation of the lunar cycle. A synodic month represents the moon's journey around the Earth in relation to the sun, and begins and ends with a new moon. A synodic month is 29.530 days.

MOON FACT

The time it takes for the moon to circle around the Earth relevant to a fixed point in the night sky and the time in which the moon rotates around its own axis is called a sidereal month. A sidereal month is 27.321 days.

Phases of the moon, engraving by P. Miotte

Even though our current calendar is based on the sun, the word we use for a period of approximately 30 days ('month' in English, 'maand' in Dutch, 'Monat' in German, based on the proto-German *mǣnóth*) reveals that we used to base our timekeeping on the moon.

Today, many cultures and religions still use the moon as guiding principle. However, these lunar calendars are not all synchronised; the day considered the first day of the month often differs. Some, like the Jewish calendar, the Islamic calendar, the Chinese calendar and the Japanese calendar, start a new month approximately with the new moon. Others start with the full moon, while a few are based on phases between the full moon and the new moon. Just to keep it simple.

Scientific views on the moon have also evolved significantly over the past twenty centuries. Aristotle believed that the moon was part of the night sky; since all celestial bodies were superior to Earth in his world view, they had to be perfectly smooth circles. Galileo Galilei changed that perspective when he pointed his telescope at the moon and sketched the satellite's surface, adding it to the groundbreaking astronomical treatise *Sidereus Nuncius* or 'Sidereal Messenger', which caused an uproar in the academic world in 1610: the moon turned out not to be perfectly smooth at all, but uneven and rough with lower-lying darker areas and lighter mountainous areas. Early astronomers believed that those differences between light and dark must be the natural boundaries of some sort of moon continents, where the darker areas had to be *lunar maria* ('moon seas'). Until well into the 19th century, people expected that the moon might be host to vegetation and life.

However, our view of the satellite took a drastic turn when interest in the moon expanded beyond astronomers and astrologers; suddenly, world leaders also wanted a piece of the action.

Fig.1.

Fig.12.

Fig.8.   Fig.9.

Fig.10.   Fig.11.

Fig.13.

Fig.2.   Fig.3.

Fig.4.   Fig.5.   Fig.6.   Fig.7.

Engraved Chiefly from Original Drawings by Kirkwood & Son Edin.r

The phases of the moon, engraving

the moon is not only beautiful
it is so far away
the moon is not only ice cold
it is here to stay

CAT POWER
The Moon

In the mid-20th century, the moon became a political asset. During the Cold War, the USA and the USSR were in a state of constant rivalry, each attempting to surpass the other to consolidate their status as world powers. Armaments and aerospace were key pawns in the global struggle for dominance.

Neil Armstrong strums a ukelele after the return of Apollo 11

THE RACE FOR SPACE
The moon as a scientific and political object

Not that those world leaders were actually interested in exploring that white-gold crescent in the sky, as such. However, space travel required a programme to develop rocket science, and rockets were considered very useful in fortifying their military position. Satellite technology also progressed in leaps and bounds, making it easier for both sides to spy on each other and keep track of any atomic bombs that might be heading their way. Quite convenient.

The first move on the space chess board was made by the Russians, when they launched the unmanned satellite Sputnik 1 into space in October 1957. That was a bitter pill for the Americans to swallow. After all, they were convinced that they had the upper hand in every area, especially after the defeats suffered by the Soviet Union on the Eastern Front during World War II. Adding insult to injury, only a month after the first satellite returned to Earth, the Soviets launched a second one, this time carrying a living creature on board. Data indicated that the dog, named Laika, survived the launch, but died seven hours later due to overheating and stress. Not a surprise at all. It wasn't the animal's suffering that most concerned the Americans, but the loss of face they suffered in the eyes of their people.

This jump-started a veritable 'space race'. The first man in space had to be an American; as Vice-President Lyndon B. Johnson would later say to President John F. Kennedy: *In the eyes of the world, first in space means first, period; second in space is second in everything.* NASA and its space programme were established in 1958, yet it was once again the USSR that beat the USA to the punch when Yuri Gagarin returned a hero from his space trip in 1961.

More than ever, the moon had become the bullseye, the coveted target for the first nation to reach and walk on this mysterious satellite that stood vigil over the sleep of every person on Earth. Six weeks after Gagarin's orbit, John F. Kennedy, then President of the United States of America, addressed the US Congress. Before the decade ended, he proclaimed, America would put a man on the moon (and bring him home safely again). He repeated that statement a year later, in a speech he gave at Rice University in Houston, Texas, speaking the iconic words: *'We choose to go to the moon in this decade and do the other things, not because they are easy, but because they are hard.'*

That does sound mighty inspirational, and many a Tumblr post might have featured this quote on a sepia background, but to Kennedy the moon was just a way to prove the superiority of the Americans – science or magic be damned. At that point, the American people had lost their initial eagerness and were no longer so supportive of these extra-terrestrial excursions that cost tons of money. But after JFK was assassinated, the Apollo programme almost became a tribute to the popular fallen leader.

Despite its fairly rocky start – in 1967 the Apollo 1 capsule went up in flames during a test launch, killing the three astronauts inside – interest in the project, and therefore the moon, remained significant. The continued interest was due in no small part to the fact that the Russians were encountering at least as many problems and starting to lag behind. On 20 July 1969, the Americans won the space race when Neil Armstrong and Buzz Aldrin stepped out onto the moon's surface to take a stroll. If you ever feel like a fifth wheel, know that Michael Collins, the third astronaut on the Apollo 11 mission, never even set foot on the moon, since somebody had to stay behind on the mothership. A matter of perspective.

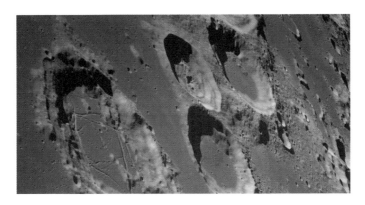

The Artemis Lander (above), ISRO Chandrayaan (middle), the lunar surface (below)

I sail to the moon
I spoke too soon
And how much did it cost
I was dropped from moonbeam
And sailed on shooting stars
Maybe you'll be president
But know right from wrong
Or in the flood you'll build an Ark
And sail us to the moon
Sail us to the moon
Sail us to the moon

RADIOHEAD
Sail to the Moon (Brush the Cobwebs out of the Sky)

Mare Orientale, a lunar mare located on the western border of the near and far side of the moon

MOON FACT

Apollo 11 almost failed to bring an American flag – the thought didn't occur to them until fairly late in the process. The astronauts had a hard time sticking the flagpole into the ground; they later said that they were petrified that the flag would fall over and hit the ground while 600 million viewers were watching. The flag did eventually fall, toppled by the blast when the spacecraft departed.

President Nixon, the leader of the USA at that time, had the honour of having 'the most historic phone call that the White House has ever had' with the moonwalkers. Armstrong, Aldrin and the ten other astronauts who took a stroll on the moon in later missions in the Apollo programme were essential to how we see the moon. During the various missions, they photographed the lunar surface and took samples for research purposes.

MOON FACT

The Apollo missions brought back about 380 kilos of lunar material with them to Earth.

That's how scientists learned that the dark lunar maria, which were believed to be some type of sea on the moon, were actually impact craters, filled with volcanic rock. In other words, the dark spots on the moon are flat plains, not seas at all. The lighter, more mountainous areas consist of a mineral that is also present in various mountain landscapes here on Earth. In addition, astronauts were also able to experience the lunar climate first-hand, telling of conditions 'as hostile as possible', with extreme temperatures. To put weather on Earth into perspective: during a lunar day, which takes two Earth weeks, the temperature can rise to over 100 °C, while temperatures at night can drop to -160 °C, since the moon does not have an atmosphere that can retain heat or disperse it across the lunar surface.

Knowing the composition of the moon's surface has helped scientists understand how the moon was formed. In 1975, astronomers William Hartman and Donald Davis published their theory that our planet was hit by a protoplanet the size of Mars soon after the solar system was created. The wandering planet that side-swiped our own was christened Theia by scientists, in honour of the mother of the moon goddess Selene.

After the collision, a piece of debris (consisting of both molten Earth and molten protoplanet) supposedly cooled down and ended up in orbit around the Earth. That hypothesis is still commonly used today, although there is no conclusive evidence that it is 100% correct. Recent study of the material that was brought back to Earth between 1969 and 1972 showed that the moon is also 150 million years older than had originally been assumed.

The more we learned about the moon, the more the satellite lost its magic for us mere mortals. The moon was 'meh', a dead, grey rock circling the Earth that was home to absolutely nothing exciting, and TV ratings for the televised rocket launches declined as a result.

The moon no longer held political interest after the space race had been decided, so President Nixon no longer saw any point in continuing the expensive battle out into the galaxy, especially since it dated back to the Kennedy presidency and was still associated with JFK. Apollo 17 in 1972 was the last mission to the moon. Despite cancelling the last three trips of the Apollo programme, Nixon left an important 'space legacy' by authorising the development of the space shuttle.

Although other presidents, including George W. Bush, did talk wistfully about conquering space again, especially the moon and Mars, there was no leader who wanted to actually foot the bill for putting those plans into practice. When the space race was at its peak, NASA was eating up more than 4% of the federal budget; by 2016 that figure was down to just half a percent.

In recent years, stargazing has been on the rise again. Not to resolve political conflicts, or answer any pressing scientific questions, or to know what time it is, but to find meaning in life, to seek comfort and to get control. The moon was recast in its mystical role and astrology returned from where the hippies had left it in the 1970s, all wrapped up in batik cheesecloth.

NEED FOR MYSTICISM
The moon as a tool for self-care and connection with nature

According to market research institute IBISWorld, the industry of palm readers, tarot readers, aura analysts and other metaphysical services grew by 2% between 2011 and 2016. The sector is currently valued at two billion dollars a year. Let that sink in for a moment.

The most important shift, though, is not the fact that interest in the moon has undergone a revival, but *who* is interested. Back in the 1970s, such New Age practices were reserved for slightly stale, flighty types who held shares in the patchouli market, but these days it's far more fashionable to occupy oneself with esotericism. From the app developer in Silicon Valley who smirkingly shares on social media that he absolutely won't date Capricorns and the influencer in your Instagram feed who had the moon tattooed on her shoulder, to the teenage girl who describes herself as a witch and thirty-somethings who celebrate the purchase of their first home by waving smoking sage in every room to cleanse the energies of their personal space: practically everyone, including your mum, is interested in astrology these days. Well, especially your mum, since she had to look up your birth certificate so you could read your astrological fingerprint right down to the minute.

After all, the astrology hype goes far beyond just looking at your horoscope in some free newspaper in the train in order to find out whether a Scorpio will or will not have a run-in with a colleague, and why an Aries should steer clear of banking matters today. Whereas most people usually know what astrological sign they are – corresponding to the position of the sun when you were born – quite a lot of people can describe their entire birth chart these days. That means that they know where planets such as Mars,

Coat by Vetements, inspired by the signs of the Zodiac

Venus and Jupiter were in the sky at the time of their birth and the influences they believe those positions had on their personality. They take the phases of the moon into account when they schedule appointments and take courses in Ayurvedic cooking. On surf and yoga vacations, they allow the waves to guide them and have local healers remove the bad energy from their bodies.

MOON FACT
The moon plays an important role in your birth chart. The position of the moon at the time of your birth determines your moon sign as well as your inner self. If your sun sign represents how you present yourself to the outside world, then your moon sign represents your subconscious, your emotions, your deepest feelings. Discover on page 157 how you can find out your moon sign and what the various signs mean.

Astrology has become part of the lifestyle of modern twenty- and thirty-somethings, and companies play that angle perfectly. Amazon sends shopping horoscopes to its Prime Insider subscribers. Mystic Lipstick, a spiritual subscription service that puts together boxes containing healing crystals, reiki bath salts and 'spiritual aids', reported a 75% increase in its subscriber base in 2017 over the year before. Even *The Cut*, the lifestyle section of the prestigious *New York Magazine*, saw clicks on their articles about horoscopes increase by 150% in 2018. Astrology apps, podcasts and vlogs popped up everywhere over the past few years (you can find a list with all of our favs on the final pages of this book). Trendy parties in New York offer a chance to have your aura photographed, while fashion brands such as Agent Provocateur, Valentino and Vetements presented collections inspired by the signs of the Zodiac. As we write this book, type in the word 'astrology' on the Urban Outfitters website and you will get 69 hits . From pillowcases printed with constellations, dowsing rods as pendants on necklaces, and T-shirts with texts like 'Scorpio Energy' to coffee mugs with lunar cycles and gorgeously designed tarot cards. Astrology is so omnipresent that we wouldn't be surprised if

Starbucks launched a StarSign Latte at some point, or if you were soon expected to buy tampons not based on your monthly flow, but based on your *monthly flow.*

The fact that you are holding this book in your hands probably already means that you are exploring mysticism yourself. You may be asking your Tinder matches about their Venus sign to figure out if you're compatible, or perhaps you've massaged toxins out of your facial pores with a rose quartz roller, possibly even postponed an important phone call because an app on your phone told you that Mercury was in retrograde, and blamed a night of bad sleep on the full moon. Or maybe you just wanted to know what all that 'moonsplaining' is about lately, why all your friends' Instagram stories are bulging with astrology memes, and why they are suddenly exclaiming 'big Taurus mood' over coffee. And it's all Donald Trump's fault.

Or maybe it is, just a little. In turbulent times packed with economic uncertainties, political upheavals and widespread polarisation in society, we are flocking to find something to hold onto, some form of comfort and control. Maybe just a simple app that says: 'Hey, it is perfectly normal that you feel drained today, but in four days there will be a new moon, and you'll have plenty of energy again after that.' Or a lifestyle that tells you what's good for you ('don't sign contracts when Mercury seems to be turning away from the sun') and why things seem bumpy between you and your loved one ('people with their moon in Aquarius are just not able to channel those types of emotions'). Banu Guler actually got the idea for Co-Star after Trump was voted into the White House, inspired by a sense that she needed to do something useful for the world – that astrology could be a bandage on the wound, a form of self-care, a simple tool in a complicated society.

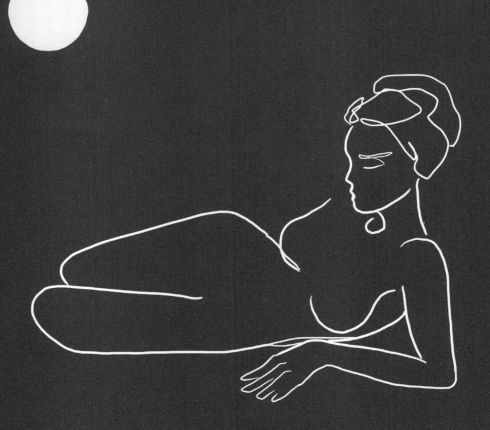

MOON FACT

'New spirituality is the new norm', WGSN predicted in its 2016 trend forecast. Trendwolves, a trend bureau in Belgium, were on the right track when they highlighted the trend towards 'mindful mind wandering': the necessity of changing our mindsets and taking a less rational approach to our living environment. JWT Intelligence in the US presented a similar story, referring to it as a desire for 'unreality'. As they explain it, it's no coincidence that now of all times sees us returning to new ways of finding meaning and purpose, repelled by the political and economic climate.

The Romantic period of the 18th century, which was characterised by introspection, emotion and intuition, was also a response to the Enlightenment and its focus on science and progress. After being bombarded with smart phones, smart televisions, smart watches, smart fabrics and even smart refrigerators, we long for things that might not have an immediate scientific explanation and return to our roots by trusting more in nature. We eat the way our early ancestors ate (palaeo), or the way our grandparents did (everything fresh from the farm). We're heading out in huge numbers to go on long walks to clear our minds, and we are suspicious of cosmetics and cleaning products that contain ingredients without a clearly identifiable origin.

○

Man shot to the moon
I bought a paperback and want to go real soon
I'm shot to the moon
Been there a half an hour,
I want to come home soon

SUN KIL MOON
Space Travel Is Boring

In addition, astrology also plays into our need for self-actualisation and identification. Contrary to what you initially imagined with tarot readers and pendulum swingers, astrologers are not (just) limited to predicting the future. Your birth chart mainly provides insights into yourself, who you are, how you act in certain situations and why certain things are easier or harder for you than for others. Having an astrologer read your birth chart – or using an app to do it – is the same as reading a book about yourself, an experience that lies somewhere between a Eureka! discovery and a round of self-masturbation. Instead of having years of therapy and picking off the psychological scabs of the past, you could also just instantly blame your commitment issues on the fact that the sun was in Sagittarius when you were born.

Just to set matters straight here: there is not a shred of scientific evidence for any causal connection between the position of the solar system and our personality, let alone the influence Mercury has on how your sweetheart interprets the number of x's under your text message. Most of the people who are interested in astrology are well aware of that. But that's irrelevant. The point isn't whether there is empirical evidence for astrology, but whether it is useful. You can believe in the power of the moon, the compatibility of certain constellations of stars, or in the healing effects of certain minerals, without having to confirm that it's true and based on proof – kind of like religion, in other words.

For centuries, that metaphysical, comforting role was exclusively reserved for the church, but traditional faiths are having a harder time finding young followers in our secular Western society. In 2017, the PEW Research Centre reported that 27% of young Americans would describe themselves as 'more spiritual than religious'. That is not surprising: the values and standards of organised religion are diametrically opposed to our neoliberal culture in which our individual freedoms are prioritised above all else.

Although our interest in traditional faith may be ebbing away, our questions about a sense of purpose and the need for something that transcends our own self have not waned. After all, people will always have an innate desire for the supernatural, for mysticism. People just love to believe in something that cannot be explained, because it lets us feel we have more control over the world. We are inclined to attribute a profound meaning to certain events: from birds flying in a specific formation to a dream we had. It's very hard for us to accept that things sometimes just happen by coincidence.

These days, we assemble our own religion as if ordering from a menu, borrowing practices from various faiths and religions. We meditate, drink tea to achieve emotional equilibrium, incorporate spiritual symbols into our accessories, and turn our gaze to the heavens, looking for answers.

The moon is a loyal companion.
It never leaves.
It's always there, watching, steadfast,
knowing us in our light and dark moments,
changing forever just as we do.
Every day it's a different version of itself.
Sometimes weak and wan,
sometimes strong and full of light.
The moon understands
what it means to be human.
Uncertain. Alone.
Cratered by imperfections.

TAHEREH MAFI
Shatter Me

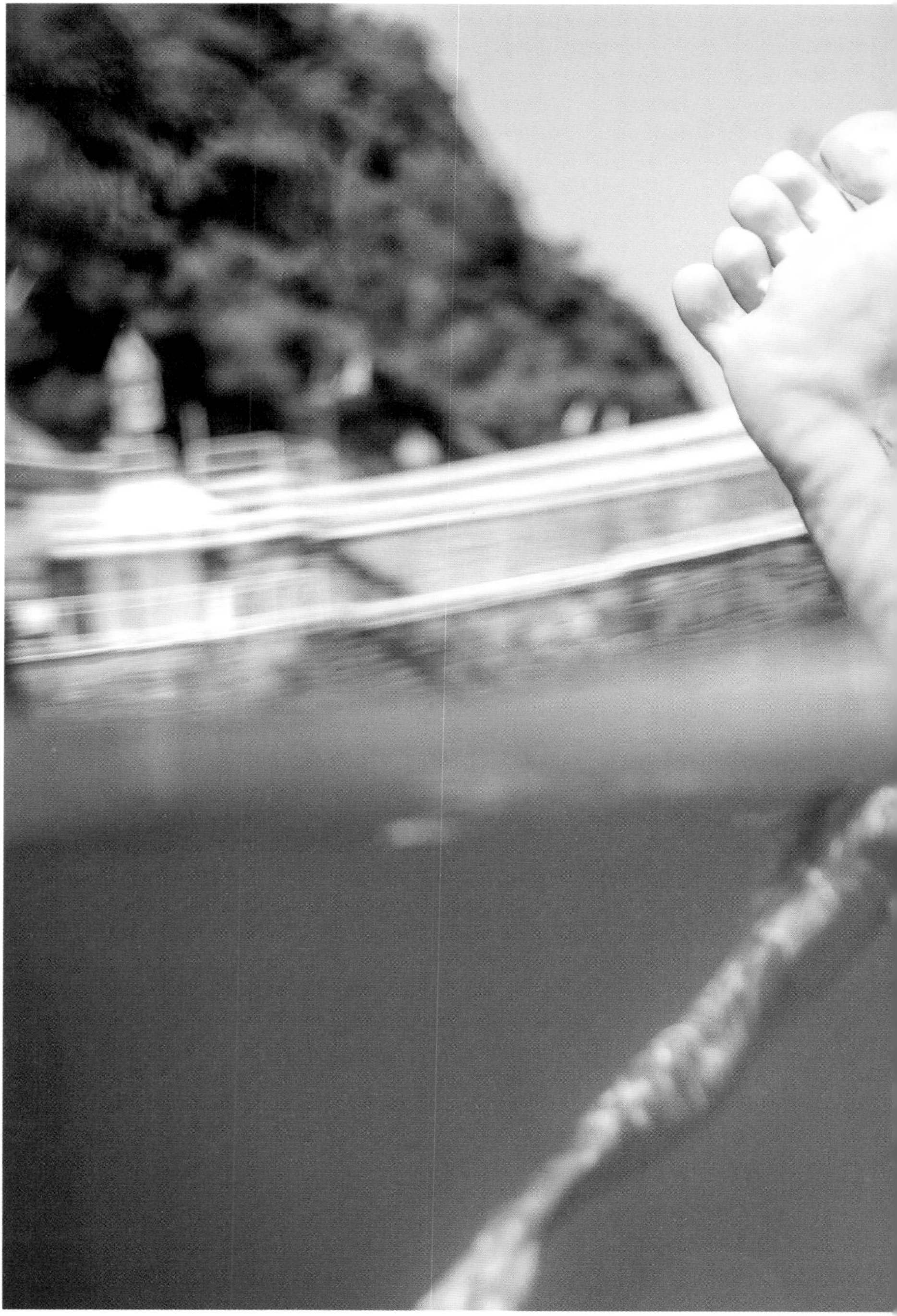

On the worldwide mission to conquer space the moon is but a pit stop. Yet interest has rekindled across the world in recent years.

THE MOON OF TOMORROW
The moon as a tourist destination and economic resource

Where his predecessors were never willing to invest enough in a new mission to the moon ('*no bucks, no Buck Rogers*'), Donald Trump did free up approximately 2 billion dollars to fund NASA's new space programme. The goal? To put people back on the moon again by 2024, including the first female astronaut. That's why the National Aeronautics and Space Administration (better known as NASA) has dubbed the project Artemis, after the goddess of the moon and twin sister to Apollo, the name used for the first missions to the moon.

Granted, Trump's ambitions stretch beyond the moon – 'been there, done that'. The main goal is Mars, but the moon has become an interesting pit stop. In 2009, NASA deliberately crashed the LCROSS satellite on the lunar surface; after analysing the dust cloud produced by the crash-landing, it proved to contain over 100 litres of frozen water. Water on the moon is estimated to account for about 1 litre per cubic metre of dust on the lunar surface. That makes the moon something more than just a dead, grey object, as people were thinking after the Apollo missions. In addition, the moon has therefore also become interesting from a logistical perspective: its water could be broken down into hydrogen and oxygen, key elements in keeping people and spacecraft operational.

MOON FACT
Obviously, it will be key to free up budget for those Moon to Mars missions, as NASA calls them. The plan is to fund the missions by continuing government support for the International Space Station (ISS) in 2025; since 2019, the American modules of the space station have been opened up for commercial purposes. Starting in 2020, 'space tourists' could spend a maximum of 30 days in the space centre. One word of caution before you start planning your Easter holidays in space: even as a commercial astronaut, you still have to pass all the medical tests and complete all the training programmes.

Starship MK1 of Elon Musk's company SpaceX

Interest in the moon has gradually rekindled across the world. Early in 2019, the Chinese managed to successfully land their Chang'e-4 spacecraft on the back of the moon (i.e. the side of the moon never visible from Earth). India, Israel and Russia have also set their sights on the moon. The European Space Agency is even considering the idea of establishing an international, permanently staffed moon village by around 2050.

The business community has had extra-terrestrial interests since the turn of the century, however. The early 21st century saw the birth of so many commercial aerospace start-ups that people began calling it a New Space movement. They wanted to make space travel cheaper and more accessible, proving their technological superiority by developing satellites, engines and instruments for NASA or even setting up their own space programmes. Billionaires Elon Musk (Tesla), Jeff Bezos (Amazon) and Richard Branson (Virgin) have all founded their own space companies with the intention of

For every human being who looks up
at the moon in the nights to come
will know that there is some corner
of another world that is forever mankind.

PRESIDENT NIXON
Last words of the alternative speech of President Nixon
in the event the Apollo II mission had failed

taking their slice of space. Why settle for being 'incredibly wealthy' when you can also be 'astronomically wealthy'?

For the next few decades, the moon will mostly be used to make 'moon money', according to the experts. For instance, the moon offers options to mine for Helium-3, a possible fuel for future fusion reactors. We are also seeing a surge in development and sales of technology and instruments that could be used in space. Back in 2007, Google launched the Google Lunar X Prize (GLXP): the technology titan was willing to pay twenty million dollars to the first private team to successfully land a robotic spacecraft on the moon and execute a few simple tasks. So far, no one has come to claim the prize. And Amazon top executive Jeff Bezos pumps a billion dollars into Blue Origin every year, in part to fund development on the Blue Moon lunar module that can be used to deliver cargo to the moon, which Bezos hopes to send along on the next Artemis mission in 2024.

The most obvious and inspirational way to monetise the moon is through space tourism, opening up the moon as a coveted destination thanks to its close proximity to Earth, the fact that it is more or less familiar territory, and the discovery of water on the moon. Many companies in the New Space movement, including Elon Musk's SpaceX, are solidly invested in that goal; by 2035, the expectation is that anyone who has the money for it will be able to secure a ride on one of these commercial 'flights'.

MOON FACT
The first space tourist who will board SpaceX for a six-day flight around the moon will be Japanese artist Yuraku Maezawa, who bought up all the seats on the first SpaceX flight. He plans to literally and figuratively take eight fellow artists to higher levels as part of the art project #dearMoon. Maezawa is convinced that the experience will be an incredible source of inspiration for the artists. Artists with extraterrestrial ambitions can still sign up for the trip, by the way. A SpaceX Starship launch including passengers is expected to take off in 2023.

Now that we are increasingly starting to see space as our playground, businesses are bursting with creativity. The foundation of most ideas is basically: what if we reinvent all the things that we find completely normal here on Earth ... but then in space! For example, Celestis lets people and their pets dream of a lunar funeral, in which the ashes of the dearly departed can be scattered on (well, considering the lower gravity, scattered over) the moon. Then there's Zero2Infinity, a Spanish company that wants to offer space tourism with balloons. Yes, you read that correctly. Balloons. Travellers would board a craft called a 'Bloon', a capsule suitable for 4 people and 2 crew members, who would then be flown to the edge of space using a helium balloon. According to the company, that would make it possible to see the edge of the Earth and the line of the planet's atmosphere before descending back to the ground by parachute. The entire event would take about four hours and put to shame pretty much any amusement park ride in the world. In a related initiative, Planetary Resources (a company that has developed a powerful telescope) would give private individuals and schools the opportunity to use the pictures that the telescope makes – for a small fee. Not as far-fetched, but if you truly invest in the project, you will get the chance to take a 'space selfie': they project a photo of you onto the telescope, and then the device takes a picture with the Earth or the moon in the background. Yes, apparently that is a thing. No, we also have no idea how far this will go.

But one thing is certain: when it comes to monetising the moon, the sky is anything but the limit.

Fly me to the moon
let me play among the stars
let me see what spring is like
on Jupiter and Mars.

FRANK SINATRA
Fly Me to the Moon

B

THE MOON
AS A MUSE

THE MOON AS A SOURCE OF INSPIRATION FOR ARTISTS, MUSICIANS AND WRITERS

As clearly and brightly as the moon hangs in the heavens, it was inevitable that it would inspire writers across the world and throughout eternity. The way that people see themselves, the world and the universe can be read pretty accurately from the literary moon at any given moment in time. The moon as a woman. The moon inside the person. The scientific moon. The melancholy moon. The moon as a mirror. The moon as a destination. And, as always, the moon as a muse. The attraction that the moon exerts on the tides is a fact, but it seems that the moon also has an inescapable pull on our imagination.

Film still of *Frau im Mond* by Fritz Lang

THE MOON IN WRITING

PLUTARCH OF CHAERONEA — *MORALIA*
(APPROX. 100 A.D.)

Galileo Galilei only unravelled the moon's mysteries at the end of 1609, when he zoomed in on it with his first telescope on top of a hill in Tuscany. However, as early as 100 A.D., the Greek philosopher Plutarch of Chaeronea was already noting observations of a scientific nature. For example, in book twelve of his essays the *Moralia*, he mentioned the face in the moon. He invented his findings about the moon's topography and lunar phases in a kind of astronomical dialogue - or what he could observe of the lunar landscape with the naked eye.

In this fashion, astronomical knowledge relied on by European writers remained limited to the musings of such philosophers as Plato and Aristotle until the 17th century. The literary moon was timeless until Galileo finally changed our perception. The introduction of heliocentrism, which challenged the assumption that the Earth was the centre of the universe, also gave lunar literature a serious boost. It became quite the art form to reconcile old myths with the growing body of scientific discoveries.

LUCIANUS OF SAMOSATA — *A TRUE STORY*
(2ND CENTURY A.D.)

In the old myths, the moon already served as a projection of the theatre of war on Earth. One example is the Greek satire authored by the Syrian philosopher Lucian of Samosata, who wrote *A True Story* in the 2nd century A.D. In essence, it was an early form of science fiction in which Lucian of Samosata described his wide-ranging journeys across the ocean. In one of the tales in his narrative, storm winds blow his ship to the moon, where he finds himself in the middle of a war between celestial bodies. The lunar entities conceived by Lucian's imagination were huge humanoid creatures dressed in woven glass, who survived by eating frogs. In his tales, the moon wasn't all that different from life on Earth.

JOHANNES KEPLER — *SOMNIUM*, OR *THE DREAM*
(1634)

The latest scientific discoveries in that era also seemed to confirm that assumption. Apparently, the moon was quite similar to our planet, with its mountains and seas. In *The Anatomy of Melancholy* (1621), Robert Burton described Galileo's observations: lighter patches of soil and shadowy seas, hills and valleys. And therefore he wondered, 'If it be so that the Earth is a moon, then are we also giddy, vertiginous and lunatic within this sublunary maze?"

That close-up of the moon was an image that continued to fascinate the German astronomer Johannes Kepler for his entire life: what would our Earth look like when viewed from atop the moon? As a student, he had a dream that he continued to develop in his *Somnium* (*The Dream*), which was published in 1634 after his death; it contained at least three times as many scientific notes and drawings. In that book, a demon transports Duracotus from Earth to the island of Levania (the moon), inhabited by monstrously huge creatures who believe that they are staring at the rotating Earth from a motionless platform – just like we had believed here on Earth for all those centuries that our planet did not move.

In 1638, barely four years later, another kidnapping story was published under the title of *The Man in the Moone, or A Discourse of a Voyage thither* by Francis Godwin. It was chock-full of recently acquired knowledge about the lunar landscape and trajectories of celestial bodies: Domingo Gonsales of Spain is carried to the moon by wild swans ('gansas').

CYRANO DE BERGERAC — *A VOYAGE TO THE MOON* (1657)

In essence, those journeys and kidnappings were introducing the moon as an exotic travel destination. More than a canvas for our earthly projections, the revelations of Copernicus and Galileo transformed the moon into a strange, possibly reachable, but above all superior new world. In *A Voyage to the Moon* (1657) by French author Cyrano de Bergerac, the protagonist makes a deliberate attempt to reach the moon by using fireworks attached to a primitive rocket. On the moon, he meets the local inhabitants and learns about magnetic flying devices and even audio books.

APHRA BEHN — *THE EMPEROR OF THE MOON* (1687)

That extraterrestrial progressiveness was also highlighted in the comedic play *The Emperor of the Moon* (1687) by English playwright Aphra Behn. Doctor Baliardo is obsessed with the moon and constantly travels to it in his imagination. To play a trick on him, his daughter's sweetheart pretends that he is the emperor of the moon, claiming that he has travelled all the way to Earth to marry her. A few convoluted scientific statements convince the father and he agrees to the marriage ... only to find out later that he is just dealing with Joe Bloggs and not a superior lunar being.

EDWARD YOUNG — *THE COMPLAINT: OR, NIGHT-THOUGHTS ON LIFE, DEATH, & IMMORTALITY* (1742)

In his lengthy poem *The Complaint: or, Night-Thoughts* (1742), Edward Young writes in nine parts or 'nights' about how the moonlight grants access to another world. Those who enter it are freed from the shackles of mortal life. Death is a portal to something superior to life, and the moon offers us a glimpse of it. Young's fusion of science and mysticism left a strong impression on Romantic artists in England, such as William Blake and Samuel Palmer.

EDGAR ALLAN POE — *THE UNPARALLELED ADVENTURE OF ONE HANS PFAALL* (1835)

In 1835, Edgar Allen Poe published the story *The Unparalleled Adventure of One Hans Pfaall* in the *Southern Literary Messenger* newspaper. In the form of a news report, Poe tells about the journey to the moon of a Rotterdam resident who travels with a balloon equipped with a machine that transforms the vacuum of space into oxygen. Fake news, to be sure, but it did introduce the scientifically and technologically substantiated idea of a journey to the moon.

Harvest Moon, Shoreham by Samuel Palmer

What then his vengeance? Hear it not, ye stars!
And thou, pale moon! turn paler at the sound;
Man is to man the sorest, surest ill.

EDWARD YOUNG
The Complaint, or, Night Thoughts, 1742

JULES VERNE — *FROM THE EARTH TO THE MOON*
(1865)

And with his popular novel *From the Earth to the Moon*, illustrated by French artist Henri de Montaut, French writer Jules Verne cashed in on the concept of the moon as a travel destination. The story dug deep, with technological, scientific and even financial details about this plausible journey to the moon. The *Columbiad*, a supercannon that was launched from Florida to the moon, even prompted the *Pall Mall Gazette* to use the word 'spaceship' for the first time in 1880.

H.G. Wells also wrote about space travels in *The First Men in the Moon* (1901). No complicated calculations this time, but a gravity-defying sphere that was catapulted to the moon. More rockets were introduced in 1929 due to Fritz Lang's film adaptation of Thea von Harbou's novel *Frau im Mond*. In that film, we follow the story of competing businessmen who travel to the moon in the rocket *Friede* in their search for gold.

ARTHUR C. CLARKE — *EARTHLIGHT*
(1955)

In the 1950s, the moon changed from just a destination for fun trips to a vehicle for political conflict as well – no longer used as a reflection of our earthly existence, but as an extension of it. In Robert A. Heinlein's young-adult science fiction novel *Rocket Ship Galileo* (1947), three teenagers explore the moon and discover a secret camp with Nazi refugees and evidence of nuclear explosions.

In Arthur C. Clarke's *Earthlight* (1955), we also recognise the tensions of the Cold War with extraterrestrial colonies and a struggle to control the natural resources beneath the moon's surface. In 1951, Clarke – who also was a physicist – had already written about the technological options of a space mission in his novel *Prelude to Space*. But obviously the writer is most famous for *2001: A Space Odyssey*, which served as the basis for the film directed by Stanley Kubrick in 1968: in the first frames of the film, we see the Earth rising above the moon and the sun rising above the Earth, aligning the three celestial bodies in one shot. The author was a familiar face on American TV, where he reported on the Apollo expeditions together with Walter Cronkite.

W.H. AUDEN — *MOON LANDING*
(1969)

With Apollo 11, the moment had finally arrived: the first people on the moon. On 20 July 1969, Neil Armstrong and Buzz Aldrin planted the American flag there. The dream became a reality, but that did not remove the reality from our dreams.

Some poets resisted this conquest. Instead of the requested laudatory poem, W.H. Auden wrote a sceptical tale in 1969. In *Moon Landing*, he heaped scorn on the macho astronauts who had experienced a 'huge phallic adventure': it would not have occurred to women, according to the poet. He understands the desire, but ultimately 'the thing is not worth going to see'. He prefers his neat and tidy garden, 'where to die has a meaning'. Fortunately, the moon survives the invasion of man and remains 'unsullied'.

MARGE PIERCY — *THE MOON IS ALWAYS FEMALE*
(1980)

Even though we cannot take that concept of 'unsullied' too literally – those first footsteps in the fine moon dust are indelible proof. It is clear that Auden's mystical moon lives on in poetry and literature. And perhaps it was indeed specifically women, as W.H. Auden writes, who would not take part in the space race. Quite literally; despite Fritz Lang's film about a woman on the moon 40 years before the actual lunar landing, we are now in 2020, and no woman has yet set foot on lunar soil.

But when women also started to write about the moon, they saw it less as a destination and more as a feminine force gazing down on Earth.However, the good-natured, feminine moon described by, amongst others, Emily Dickinson and Louisa May Alcott was nowhere to be found in *The Moon Is Always Female* by American poet Marge Piercy. Here the moon serves to illustrate the struggle of women to find their place in a world where their voice is cut off:

For the uses of men we have been butchered
and crippled and shut up and carved open
under the moon that swells and shines
and shrinks again into nothingness, pregnant
and then waning toward its little monthly
death. The moon is always female but the sun
is female only in lands where females
are let into the sun to run and climb.

MARGE PIERCY
The Moon Is Always Female, 1980

If the moon smiled, she would resemble you.
You leave the same impression
Of something beautiful, but annihilating.
Both of you are great light borrowers.
Her O-mouth grieves at the world;
yours is unaffected.

SYLVIA PLATH
The Rival, 1962

SIMON ARMITAGE — *CONQUISTADORS*
(2019)

With his first poem as England's brand-new poet laureate, Simon Armitage reflected on how he experienced that landing on the moon fifty years ago as a little child. He was inspired by such influences as writer Robert Graves, who was shocked by the 'muddy footprints' on the 'maternal, feminist goddess' and who called Aldrin and Armstrong's walk on the moon a 'crime against humanity'. Auden would nod in approval.

In this afterthought
he's just turned six,
the astronaut in him
doing his damnedest to coincide
the moon landing
with his first kiss,
hoping to plant his lips
on _____ 's
distant face
as Simon Armstrong
steps from the module
onto Tranquillity Base.
But as Tricky Dicky clears his throat
to claim God's estate
as man's backyard
from the Oval Office,
and the gap narrows
to feet then inches,
suddenly stars recoil
to the next dimension
and heaven flinches.

SIMON ARMITAGE
Conquistadors, 2019

As the tranquil evening moon
Looks on that restless sea,
So a mother's gentle face,
Little child, is watching thee.

LOUISA MAY ALCOTT
The Mother Moon, 1856

The stars about the lovely moon
Fade back and vanish very soon,
When, round and full, her silver face
Swims into sight, and lights all space.

SAPPHO
Greek poet, 6th Century A.D.

With or without a telescope: the eyes of the astronomer and the artist are both focused on the same moon, sparking everyone's imagination. In an attempt to grab hold of that elusive moon, we have all pointed our smartphone to the sky at some time in an attempt to commemorate that moment, only to have captured a lamentable spot of light that might as well have been a streetlight. Fortunately, we had and have talented artists in our midst who have managed to capture the versatile character of the moon on canvases throughout history.

THE MOON IN PAINTING

THE CAVES OF LASCAUX — UNKNOWN
(APPROXIMATELY 15,000 B.C.)

Our prehistoric ancestors had already expressed their admiration for the moon on rock walls. The caves of Lascaux in France are where art was born. And if you look closely, alongside the depictions of primitive horses and deer adorning the wall, you can also see a remarkable system of dots. It represents a 17,000-year-old lunar calendar, according to scientists, that was used to map the arrival and departure of our planet's satellite in the night sky. No art without the moon, in other words.

In County Meath, Ireland, we find another moon map: carved into a 5,000-year-old tomb in such a way that, at certain times, moon shines in, lighting up the map, as it continues its trajectory across the sky. In Celtic legend, the moon aided the Celts by guiding their souls to the afterlife. Similar stories were told by the ancient Egyptians. In depictions of the god Khonsu ('the traveller'), we can see how he balances the protective moon on his head while guiding souls to the afterlife.

THE NEBRA SKY DISC — UNKNOWN
(APPROXIMATELY 1600 B.C.)

More proof of our ancient fascination with the moon was forged in 1600 B.C. *The Nebra Sky Disc* is a sculpture of metal and gold, 30 cm wide. Scientists believe it would have served an astronomical purpose, as it was not unusual for certain cultures in the Bronze Age to keep a close eye on the sky. It seems the artist even managed to re-create the rough surface of the moon that was visible to the naked eye.

JAN VAN EYCK — *THE CRUCIFIXION AND LAST JUDGEMENT*
(1430-1440)

For a long time, it was assumed that Leonardo da Vinci was the first to document the textures of the lunar landscape in his many sketches, a century before the first telescope was invented. But even if we exclude the ingenuity of the celestial disc that pre-dated it by thousands of years and focus exclusively on paintings, there would still be someone who beat Da Vinci to it. The master of the Flemish Primitives, Jan van Eyck, depicted the waning moon most accurately in his diptych *The Crucifixion and Last Judgement*, painted between 1430 and 1440 – decades before Da Vinci's writings saw the light of day. We see the moon somewhere in the top right corner of the piece, resembling a skull floating in the twilight behind the crucifixion of three figures. The terminator is visible, as well as the largest lunar mare: a detailed observation of the moon at dawn's light.

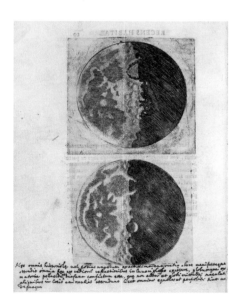

Hæc omnis huiusmodi uel penius negatiuæ apparebunt inaqualis, clare non supercape...
ostendis omnia hæc ex redioru refractionibus in lunam globo oriens, ...
natoria pilleris...rediciam conficium ese, que non album ab globi instituti maculati...
aliquibus in locis eminentis ostendant. Quod omnino aquilus et perfoliti sine ...
Sapraque

DIEGO VELÁZQUEZ — THE IMMACULATE CONCEPTION (1618-1619)

Van Eyck's moon observations are remarkable, since up to the Renaissance the Church had generally considered the moon to be a clear crystal ball for Mary to rest on along her way to heaven. Much like in one of Velázquez's oldest known works, *The Immaculate Conception*, which depicts a young woman – the mother of Jesus – standing on a nearly transparent moon with a halo of twelve stars around her head. It would be among the last of such depictions of the moon in the aftermath of Galileo's revelations.

GALILEO GALILEI — SIDEREUS NUNCIUS (1610)

Galileo stated that the moon was illuminated by the sun's light reflecting off the Earth's surface, thus laying the foundations for a heliocentric view of the solar system. When he looked at the moon through his telescope, he saw it in all its complexity: Galilei was both a scholar and an artist, and he painted the moon in watercolours. He depicted the newly discovered lunar landscape by adding shadows and lights, craters and seas, and published his illustrations in the widely distributed *Siderius Nuncius*. The secrets of the moon were revealed. But even though the moon in Galileo's pictures suddenly looked far more like Earth, and that representation found its way into art, the symbolism generally remained separate from the science.

JOSEPH WRIGHT OF DERBY —
AN EXPERIMENT ON A BIRD IN THE AIR PUMP
(1768)

The moon takes on many forms in our imagination and its meaning is layered. Take, for instance, *An Experiment on a Bird in the Air Pump* (1768) by English painter Joseph Wright of Derby. We catch only a glimpse of the bright full moon, half obscured and viewed through a window. It is a classic poetic device and a way to bring contrast into the work – but also includes a sly reference to the Lunar Society that Wright also belonged to. This group of scientists convened every month on the Sunday closest to the full moon, to discuss scientific and societal progress. The moon was viewed as a symbol for wisdom, certainly, but also as a highly necessary beacon of light that the members of the club trusted to illuminate their path.

WILLIAM BLAKE — *I WANT! I WANT!*
(1793)

The moon also symbolises desire and flight. A destination, within reach or beyond our grasp. We can see it in Montaut's illustration for the cover of Verne's novel *From the Earth to the Moon*. It is also visible in William Blake's engraving *I Want! I Want!* (1793): smaller than a playing card, depicting an early fantasy about a journey to the moon. A child-like figure has a similarly child-like solution, putting up a large ladder to reach the moon.

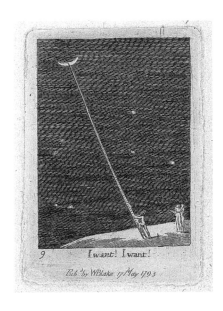

CASPAR DAVID FRIEDRICH —
MAN AND WOMAN CONTEMPLATING THE MOON
(1818)

We already saw it in the ancient Egyptians and Celts, and in the shining path of the Lunar Society: the moon in a guiding role. In Romanticism, the moon takes on a slightly more mysterious meaning as a symbol for contemplation. German painter Caspar David Friedrich created a number of variants on figures staring in wonder at the unknown, unattainable moon; the first was *Two Men Contemplating the Moon*. In the similar tableau of *Man and Woman Contemplating the Moon* (1818), the moon occupies a reassuring position. We see two partners lost in thought, almost meditatively. And between the intertwining branches of the trees, the calm moon presents itself.

VINCENT VAN GOGH — *THE STARRY NIGHT*
(1889)

In a similar mood, we can also see the moon in one of its most famous depictions: *The Starry Night* by Vincent van Gogh. His moon was the moon that shone into his bedroom at the psychiatric hospital in Saint-Rémy-de-Provence. It is the only stable element in a dance of brush strokes. A moon that strikes deep to the core of your inner being, a feeling that practically everyone will have experienced at some point under the bright moonlight on a dark night.

From the position of the stars in relation to Venus and the constellation of Aries prominently displayed in the night sky, we can deduce that the moon was three-quarters full when Van Gogh painted this piece. Yet he chose to paint a crescent moon; art historian Lauren Soth has argued that it 'was intended as an image of consolation'. Another art historian, Albert Boime, discerns the

original, fuller form of the moon in the haze surrounding the crescent. Boime believes that *The Starry Night* reveals Van Gogh's interest in such things as the writings of Jules Verne, as well as his belief in an afterlife on the celestial bodies, a reflection of the astronomical progress that he experienced during his lifetime.

ALBERT JULIUS OLSSON — *RISING MOON, ST IVES BAY, CORNWALL* (EARLY 20TH CENTURY)

Throughout the centuries, many artists have tried their hand at capturing the moonlight in a couple of brushstrokes. We can safely say that the English-Swedish painter Albert Julius Olsson succeeded. The sailor knew the sea like the back of his hand, and the moon plays a prominent role at sea. During his stay in St Ives in Cornwall, England, he taught many artists. His house became an art school and studio, and was later the St Eia Hotel until 2014; the residence overlooked the port of the tiny coastal town to the north and Carbis Bay to the east, two views that frequently featured in Olsson's work.

JOAN MIRÓ — *DOG BARKING AT THE MOON* (1926)

The moon is an often-recurring element in the works of the Surrealists, reflecting their fascination with the dream world. Miró signed the manifesto of the Surrealist movement in 1924 and was even called 'the greatest Surrealist of us all' by their leader, André Breton.

The original piece had speech bubbles conveying a conversation in Catalan between the moon and the dog. 'Bow wow', the dog yelped in the original sketch as the moon looked down on it pitilessly: 'You know, I don't give a damn.' The words were erased in the final painting, but their meaning is still tangible in the lonely night and the longing that originates from the distance between various elements and the ladder that leads into nothingness.

LUIS BUÑUEL AND SALVADOR DALÍ — *UN CHIEN ANDALOU* (1929)

Over dinner in a restaurant, Buñuel told Dalí about a dream in which a cloud sliced the moon in two like a razor blade through an eye. It became the opening scene of *Un Chien Andalou*, a film based on the idea of suppressed feelings: a man sharpens his knife on a balcony while staring at the moon, which almost disappears behind a wisp of cloud. Cut to a young woman who is held by the same man staring straight ahead as he brings the knife to her eye. Cut to the moon hiding behind the cloud. Cut to a literal cut of a knife slicing through an eye of an animal – or the woman's eye.

PAUL DELVAUX — *A SIREN IN FULL MOONLIGHT* (1940)

Other examples of Surrealists who eagerly incorporated the moon in their works were Belgian artists René Magritte and Paul Delvaux. Introducing dreamy and absurd elements in their work, they tried to bring a superior reality to life. In Magritte's masterpiece, for instance, we can see various crescent moons resting on bowler hats. Delvaux was no stranger to dreamy scenes either, often with an emphasis on divinely gorgeous women and architectural details under the eerily haunting glow of the moon.

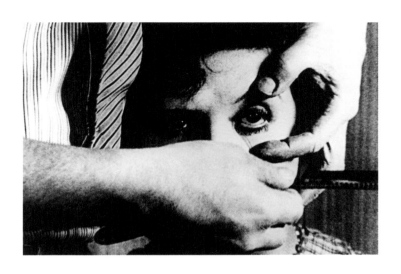

PAUL VAN HOEYDONCK — *FALLEN ASTRONAUT* (1971)

Though Aldrin, Collins and Armstrong brought the moon significantly closer to home, it still remained a distant dream for most of us. The same applies to the many artists who used the moon as their source of inspiration. Not Belgian artist Paul Van Hoeydonck: his *Fallen Astronaut* was left behind in the lunar dust by the Apollo 15 mission in honour of fourteen astronauts and cosmonauts who had perished. The 8.5-cm aluminium statue will never leave the moon again, but also symbolises that, for many of us, the moon remains unattainable.

CRISTINA DE MIDDEL — *AFRONAUTS* (2014)

For her work *Afronauts*, photographer Cristina De Middel was inspired by a space programme started by a teacher in Zambia. However, due to a lack of financial support, the country had to concede the 'space race' to the United States and the USSR. In her work, De Middel reconstructs that era's dream of the first African on the moon. The line between dream and reality fades, showing a colourful, surreal perspective in photorealistic clarity.

It is not just wolves who feel compelled to howl at the moon; people's vocal cords are also enticed to enthusiastic expression when they face Lady Luna. There are a ton of famous songs that have 'Moon' in the title, including Nick Drake's 'Pink Moon', Van Morrison's 'Moondance', or 'Moon River' by Andy Williams, used in the film *Breakfast at Tiffany's*. However, these songs are not specifically inspired by the moon; rather, the celestial body is metaphorical, much like its appearances in poetry and literature, or used to emphasise a romantic scene. In opera, moonlight or the sudden appearance of a moon in the sky is used to visually show that a character is turning insane.

THE MOON IN SONG

In this chapter we wanted to single out a few examples of music culture that have been directly inspired by the natural satellite, or at least have a special connection with it. Didn't make the list, since it's not a song but a dance: Michael Jackson's moonwalk.

BEETHOVEN — 'MONDSCHEINSONATE'
(1801)

We are immediately off to a false start. Beethoven's fourteenth sonata is one of his most famous works, but the virtuoso himself never referred to his composition as the 'Moonlight Sonata'. A few years after Beethoven's death, music critic Ludwig Rellstab reflected in an article that the first part of the sonata reminded him of the way the moonlight shone over Lake Lucerne, an image that struck such a nerve with the public that it stuck. What Beethoven would personally have thought about the alternative title, we will never know – but it does sound much catchier than the incredibly dry 'Piano Sonata No. 14 in C# minor, Opus 27 No. 2'. This is a perfect example of how the moon can capture the imagination, even though that was not the composer's initial intent.

FRANK SINATRA — 'FLY ME TO THE MOON'
(1964)

Maybe a bit too obvious, but not many people know that this jazzy song had already seen the light of day in 1954 by the hand of Bart Howard under the title 'In Other Words', because the 1964 cover by Frank Sinatra, dubbed 'Fly Me to the Moon' for convenience's sake, became much more famous. Not just because Sinatra, aka 'Old Blue Eyes', was a superstar, but also because this song could have been heard by any alien ears out there. The hit song was played by the astronauts on Apollo 10's flight around the moon, and several months later on the moon itself by Buzz Aldrin, the second man to set foot on the celestial body.

DAVID BOWIE — 'SPACE ODDITY'
(1969)

Of course this one is essential on the list. Bowie wrote this song after he, like the rest of the world, had seen the iconic photo of Apollo 8 astronaut Bill Anders, the first person to circle the moon in a manned spacecraft. 'Space Oddity' tells the tale of 'Major Tom', an astronaut who is abandoned in space, 'floating around in my tin can, far above the moon.' A few years later, Bowie would explain in more detail that the song was a comment on what he saw were the limits of American exceptionalism. 'Here we had the great blast of American technological know-how shoving this guy up into space, but once he gets there, he's not quite sure why he's there. And that's where I left him.'

Ingeniously, Bowie's single was launched five days after the Apollo 11 mission lifted off, making it the unofficial soundtrack of the space race and

the signature song for stargazers. The title was of course based on Stanley Kubrick's masterpiece, *2001: A Space Odyssey*. Over the next few years, Bowie would expand his fascination for space through his alter ego Ziggy Stardust and the alien Starman, and the character of Major Tom also returned several times in his *oeuvre*.

In 2013, Canadian astronaut Chris Hadfield recorded his own version of 'Space Oddity' from orbit, with Bowie's consent, and when the SpaceX Falcon Heavy rocket took the Tesla Roadster personally owned by CEO Elon Musk along into space in 2017, 'Space Oddity' was one of the songs that was played on repeat through the car's sound system. An additional detail: the mannequin that was placed behind the wheel was given the name Starman, another tribute to Bowie.

PINK FLOYD — 'MOONHEAD'
(1969)

Wait ... What? Not a song from the *Dark Side of the Moon* LP? Or 'Brain Damage', the song that gave us the phrase and later the title of the 1973 record album? That would have been too obvious. And not entirely correct, either. According to songwriter Roger Waters, this 'dark side of the moon' represented dark emotions rather than celestial bodies. 'I'll see you on the dark side of the moon' means: sometimes I also wrestle with these demons and you are not alone, as he would explain later on in the book *Bricks in the Wall*.

'Moonhead', on the other hand, does have a direct connection with the moon (and the moon landing). On the night of 20 July 1969, the BBC had a special broadcast to celebrate the impending walk on the moon. David

Gilmour, Roger Waters, Nick Mason and Richard Wright had been commissioned by the BBC to compose and improvise a song live on TV to celebrate this astronomical event. Seven and a half minutes later, 'Moonhead' was born.

MOON FACT

As we have already written, the moon does not actually have a 'dark side', just the other side of the moon that we never get to see from Earth. And the moon does not radiate its own light, but is illuminated by the sun and reflects the sun's rays. Of course Pink Floyd knew that as well. If you listen to the *Dark Side of the Moon* LP all the way to the end, you'll hear Gerry O'Driscoll, the doorman of the Abbey Road Studios where the album was recorded, say, 'There is no dark side of the moon, really. Matter of fact, it's all dark.'

The song never became quite as famous as the songs from the *Dark Side of the Moon* LP. In 1969, Pink Floyd was still more of an underground band, and David Bowie and his 'Space Oddity' had actually stolen the spotlight (or rather: the moonlight) on that summer evening in the 1960s. Bootlegs of 'Moonhead' sometimes appeared online, often wrongly credited as 'Trip to Mars', but it was only in 2016 that the song was officially released on *The Early Years 1965–1972*.

MOON FACT

When MTV was launched in 1981, the music channel wanted to use the iconic images of the landing on the moon, where they would replace the American flag with one that displayed their own logo, combined with the legendary line that Neil Armstrong spoke in that moment: 'One small step for man, one giant leap for mankind.' When they asked Armstrong's permission to use the soundbite, he reportedly responded with a resounding 'Are you crazy?.' They did eventually end up using the idea for the images, but they bleeped out the Armstrong quote.

BRIAN ENO — 'AN ENDING (ASCENT)' (1983)

'An Ending' is the highlight of Brian Eno's ninth studio album. *Apollo: Atmospheres and Soundtracks* was released in 1983 as the soundtrack for the documentary *For All Mankind* by Al Reinert, featuring the Apollo lunar missions. In the liner notes, Brian Eno stated that, when watching the lunar landing in 1969 on television, he was astounded to see how this historic event had been produced for TV viewing. According to Eno, the low-resolution images and the chattering of the reporters added a melodramatic note to what could have been a beautiful moment. It was one of the main reasons why the British composer would later on devote himself to ambient music. 'An Ending' was composed with precisely that lunar landing in mind.

SMASH MOUTH — 'ALL STAR'
(1999)

You'll never know if you don't go / You'll never shine if you don't glow. These are lyrics that might indeed be about the moon, but the universally hated and celebrated hit by Smash Mouth made the list for an entirely different reason. Colin Fries, who worked in the NASA archives, had the brilliant idea a couple of years ago to collect all the 'wake-up calls' that were used for the astronauts. On the first missions, the astronauts were woken up with updates and news of the day, but during the 1970s the space crusaders were nudged from their beds with a tune of their choice, which they, their team members or their family could request.

The list includes some obvious choices: a large selection of jazz and classical music, and 'What a Wonderful World' by Louis Armstrong is notably (but unsurprisingly) prevalent, but it also contains a few unexpected gems. 'I Believe I Can Fly' by R Kelly, for example, or 'True' by Spandau Ballet. 'All I Wanna Do' by Sheryl Crowe and 'Blue' by Eiffel 65 have also been blasted from the speakers in space. Even forgotten songs such as 'Space Cowboy' by N*Sync and 'Moon and Back' by Savage Garden were taken off the dusty shelves. And so, on 10 September 2000, the dreams of the STS-106 crew were rudely interrupted by the strains of 'All Star' by Smash Mouth. Gooooood morning spacecraft!

MOON FACT

For the new lunar mission in 2024, NASA wants to create a playlist to wake up the crew members of the Artemis shuttle and accompany them on their three-day trip. Suggestions can be sent via Twitter, using the hashtag #NasaMoonTunes

BJÖRK — 'MOON'
(2011)

Björk, the famous singer from Iceland, is of course no stranger to folklore, mythology and references to nature. Her album *Biophilia* has ten songs, each of them a tribute to a certain natural phenomenon. In 'Moon', as the song's title suggests, Björk sings about the effects of the lunar cycle on Earth and plays with themes such as rebirth and energy. 'With each new moon we complete a cycle and are offered renewal – to take risks, to connect with other people, to love, to give,' as Björk herself said about the song in 2012.

KING KRULE — 'THE CADET LEAPS'
(2017)

See, we could also have included 'Walking on the Moon' by the Police in this list, because, right there is the word 'moon' in the title, and the music video was recorded in the Kennedy Space Center. But Sting has already stated that he was primarily using the moon in a more poetic context, and that he wasn't necessarily inspired by the astronauts' walk on the moon. No, we'd rather pay tribute to Archy 'King Krule' Marshall, a young British punkjazz and triphop artist who has intertwined the influence of the moon and the tides pretty much throughout his entire *oeuvre*. And not in a corny way, either. Take, for instance, the creative, funny way he juggles words in the song 'Biscuit Town', the opening song of his album *The Ooz. You're shallow waters, I'm the deep seabed / And I'm the reason you flow / I got more moons wrapped around my head and Jupiter knows / Whilst you orbit with some stupider hoes*

The third studio album by King Krule since his debut album *6 Feet beneath the Moon*, *The Ooz* was translated into a 30-minute short film titled *Live on the Moon*, in which Archy Marshall and the Molten Jets play a couple of songs from the album in actual spacesuits. The set closes with 'The Cadet Leaps'. *Above and beyond / On the rooftop / The space cadet walks through the sky / Lost in the search for distant forms of life/ Lucifer's dream /No one could hold me down*

ARCTIC MONKEYS — *TRANQUILITY BASE HOTEL & CASINO* (2018)

The sixth studio album by Arctic Monkeys may not sound spacey, but the inspiration certainly was intergalactic. The album was named after the location where the Apollo 11 lunar module landed in the dust for the first time. Astronaut Neil Armstrong announced the landing with the words: 'Houston, Tranquility Base here. The Eagle has landed.'

Arctic Monkeys frontman Alex Turner has mentioned regularly that he is a stargazer. He has collected various Apollo gadgets, and has now also named an album after the most iconic walk in history. The 'hotel and casino' part refers to the space-age hotel that is a setting in Stanley Kubrick's *2001: A Space Odyssey*. The title song of the album also has this beautiful lyric: *Technological advances / Really bloody get me in the mood/ Pull me in close on a crisp eve, baby / Kiss me underneath the moon's side boob.*

95

THE POWER
OF THE MOON

HOW THE MOON INFLUENCES LIFE ON EARTH

'The moon made me do it.'

The moon is to blame. We state it as an obvious fact when we cry watching a rom-com or go crazy to our mother's old Barry White LP. When we cannot find any other reason for our bone-numbing fatigue or exuberant enthusiasm. When parents already brace themselves for the inevitable cycle and the effect on their small children, as if they were werewolves. 'It must be the full moon, right?' Those words have been used throughout the centuries by even the most rational minds in an attempt to explain any strange behaviour or events. We look up to the night sky and, bathing in the light of our lonely satellite, we find our answers for the inexplicable.

What made people blame those things on the moon, all those centuries ago? Not only lycanthropy (the mental affliction in which someone is under the delusion that they will change into an animal) was attributed to the moon at a certain time, but ancient Greek and Roman scholars and philosophers also blamed matters such as epilepsy and other 'weird' behaviour on it. According to Pliny the Elder and Claudius Ptolemy, who lived in the 1st century A.D., man's abnormal behaviour was caused by the influence of the moon on the waters of our brains, comparable to the morning dew – but also the tides. In the 16th century, the alchemist and astrologist Paracelsus wrote about *spiritus vitae cerebri* and *spiritus sensitivus*, discussing the magnetic force of the moon: how we are attracted to the moon much like the needle of a compass is drawn to the north pole. During the English Renaissance, also known as the Shakespearean era, art and literature started to link the lunar phases to sexual urges (lunacy!), bad dreams and hallucinations.

The moon that drives us to madness: already embedded in the Latin word *lunaticus*, it found its way into the English language and even into the title of this book: *Lunatic*. In essence, 'lunatic' means moon-sick ... or insane. It became commonplace in the medical world when Sir William Blackstone introduced an actual definition for it in the 18th century: 'A LUNATIC, or *non compos mentis*, is one who has had understanding, but by disease, grief, or other accident has lost the use of his reason. A lunatic is indeed properly one that has lucid intervals; sometimes enjoying his senses, and sometimes not, and that frequently depending upon the change of the moon.'

From that point on, lunacy was more than just moon-sickness. Even though the results of the many and various studies of the moon's influence haven't exactly been verifiable, we still attribute mystical powers to our planet's satellite that contribute to suicide, menstrual cycles, babies born under a full moon, crimes by moonlight, murders, traffic accidents, more hospital admittances, dog bites and so on.

It shouldn't surprise anyone that this fascination has even made its way into scientific research. After all, the moon visibly influences the Earth in a variety of ways. The first and most prominent one is that of the moon-light: every 29.5 days we are subjected to a full moon and 14.8 days after that we get to (not) see the new moon. Then there is also the gravitational pull of the moon that leads to the tides in our oceans. Low tide and high tide alternate every 12.4 hours. At the full and new moon, when the sun, Earth and moon are aligned, high tide is higher and low tide is lower; this is known as spring tide (unrelated to the seasons!). At the first and last quarter of the moon, when the tidal forces of the sun and the moon weaken each other instead of reinforcing the pull of gravity, tides are more moderate; this is known as neap tide. Finally, another force may also be associated with the moon: 'Oceans are electrical conductors because they are made up of saltwater, and considering how they move with the tides, it also involves a magnetic field,' as Robert Wickes, space weather expert at University College London, explained to the BBC. The magnetic effect is probably minimal.

However, the moon affects our world strongly enough that people have found sufficient cause to explain our misconduct. If we note that the ratio of water to organic and inorganic solid matter in the human body is comparable to the ratio of water to solid mass in the world (approximately four to one), then shouldn't this also lead to surging tides inside the human body? Add a dash of electrolytic and hormonal fluctuations to that toxic cocktail and you are bound to end up with an emotional mess. A whole range of explanations is also attributed to biorhythms. Considering that circadian cycles (biorhythms that last about a day) and annual rhythms are widespread in the plant and animal kingdoms, and that many species also live by the rhythms of the moon and the tides, would it be that far-fetched to believe that monthly biological cycles occur in both men and women? After all, as a species, humans are about 60% water ... Cucumbers and to-matoes might suffer a stranger fate, since they are 96 and 94 percent water respectively. Are they also at the mercy of the moon's influence? Has anyone ever investigated that?

The power of the moon is undisputed. The effects of our planet's solitary satellite on nature and the living creatures around us are similarly clear. Sadly, studies that try to shed light on how the moon affects humans are often based on shaky ground. What we believe may not be absolutely impossible, but the scientific research to support it is still too limited at this point. Even so, here's a peek at what we do know.

With freedom, flowers, books, and the moon, who could not be perfectly happy?

OSCAR WILDE

MOON FACT

Werewolves have always captivated hearts and minds. We can find references for them dating back to the nearly 4,000-year-old Babylonian epic of Gilgamesh, in which a goddess changes a shepherd into a wolf. More than 2,000 years ago, Ovid told a similar story in his *Metamorphoses*, and Petronius also had some things to share about it with his Roman audience. The idea of man howling at the moon like a wolf persisted well into the Middle Ages. Not that transformation into a werewolf was always attributed to the moon. You could be cast into that dire fate by falling under a curse, by eating the wrong herbs, or by drinking water that had previously been touched by a wolf's muzzle. But by extension, you could have also contracted it if your parents had conceived you under a new moon, or if you had fallen asleep under a full moon on a Friday. And for some reason, those last examples are the ones that we continue to remember when we think about werewolves and lunacy.

It's a supernatural delight
Everybody's dancing in the moonlight

TOPLOADER
Dancing in the moonlight

In times long past, before artificial light polluted our skies, the light of the full moon would have kept us awake at night, resulting in sleep deprivation and, in some people, even leading to psychological problems. A study published in 1999 in the *Journal of Affective Disorders* suggested that connection. The study even speculated that this partial sleep deprivation would have been sufficient to cause mania or hypomania in bipolar patients.

A major review in 2014 by the Max Planck Institute for Psychiatry looking at many different studies on sleep and lunar cycles did not reveal any statistically relevant correlations. However, two years later, another study involving 5,800 children between the ages of nine and eleven from twelve different countries showed that they slept five minutes less during nights when the moon was full. Not that those few minutes would have a major impact on our health, but it is an interesting result that might signify that moonlight does affect our sleeping pattern.

That effect may be debatable, but consider how much light pollution we're exposed to on a daily basis. And then there is the question whether the results of the study can be verified by a control study.

Moonlight may not always have the most pleasant influence on our state of mind. To enjoy a good night's sleep, we should be hesitant about welcoming the moon into our home. But other life forms on Earth have different opinions: plants and animals – under water and above – take eager advantage the moon's cool glow and seem to be especially fond of moonlight to set the mood for their 'sexcapades' – although we might agree with that as well.

One of the most curious phenomena in that respect is the large-scale moon-driven ejaculation in the Great Barrier Reef of Australia. Every year in December, hundreds of coral species simultaneously release their seed into the reef waters. Various factors play a role in the timing of the entire event, such as nutrition, temperature and the salinity of the seawater, but the amount of moonlight seems to be the primary trigger. When the light is exactly right, the corals synchronously spit out millions of spermatozoa and eggs into the water to increase the chance of fertilisation. Hundreds of coral species in reefs around the globe do the same, from Hawaii and Okinawa all the way to the Caribbean, but the Australian spectacle is probably the most beautiful: it is visible from the coast as waving pink plumes in the water. A 2007 study on *Acropora millepora* explains the phenomenon: the sea creatures possess the CRY2 protein, which detects light and is exceptionally sensitive to the blue wavelengths so characteristic of moonlight. In animals, the cryptochrome proteins CRY2 and CRY1 play an important role in calibrating their internal biological clock.

It's not just animals, either; some plants are also literally aroused by moonlight. Plants usually just release their pollen into the wind, but *Ephedra foeminea*, a shrub found in the Mediterranean region, secretes sugary droplets under the full moon in July that will in turn absorb the pollen from visiting insects. According to Professor Catarina Rydin and her student Kristina Bolinder from the University of Stockholm, that timing is not coincidental. In a study published in *Biology Letters* in 2015, the two researchers found that the pollination droplets glistening in the moonlight were a key part of the plant's reproduction, beckoning seductively to lure in the pollinators.

In other cases, the effect of the moonlight is slightly less spectacular. For instance, certain bird species communicate in different ways depending on the light. Horned owls use their white neck feathers to communicate signals at night, but they become more 'talkative' during the full moon, because those light-coloured feathers are more clearly visible in bright moonlight.

In contrast, scorpions are less fond of that lunar spotlight. The UV wavelengths contained in moonlight react with a protein in their exoskeleton which gives them an almost neon blue glow. It gives these glow-in-the-dark arachnids a valid reason to scurry into hiding when the moon is full. Scorpions are therefore more active during the darkness of the new moon, which makes sense since prey animals also actively shun bright lights.

When the full moon drenches the world in bright light and chases predators into the shadows, it does make it much harder for prey animals to sate their hunger. It could even lead to food shortages for certain predator species such as lions, who prefer to hunt at night. These predators may come up empty when hunting in bright moonlight, but they usually make up for it in the days following the full moon by hunting during the daytime.

Finally, other animals and insects also make use of the moon to navigate when they set out into the wide world. For instance, the large yellow underwing moth uses the moon's azimuth (or horizontal angle) as an orientation cue to determine its flight path. The same talent is also used by other creatures, such as sand fleas. Similarly, newly hatched sea turtles use the reflection of the moon off the water's surface to guide them as they traverse the sandy beach on their way to the sea. However, light pollution could potentially disrupt these natural cycles and confuse plants and animals.

THE TIDES

You leave with the tide
And I can't stop you leaving

THE XX
Tides

The dance of the revolving Earth, sun and moon makes the water dance in tune below. Some species of oysters open and close in conjunction with lunar phases and water levels, sea turtles surf on the tide to lay their eggs higher on the beach, and ecosystems along coastlines all over the world and even beyond seem to have adapted to or rely on the periodic rise and fall of the ocean waters: the tides.

These are the large-scale events that we see in our oceans on a daily basis. This effect isn't actually about the water itself, however: tides are created by the difference in gravitational pull on one side of an object – for instance our planet – relative to the pull on the other side. In our oceans, for example, this effect takes place because the moon pulls harder on the water mass facing it, compared to the lesser pull it exerts on the Earth's core. This relative difference leads to high tide. At the same time, on the other side of the Earth, we see a stronger pull on the planet's core than on the oceans facing away from the moon: a negative force pulling the Earth away from the ocean. This is because the effects of gravity diminish with distance, but never disappear entirely. As a result, we see the tides ebb and flow every 12.4 hours, turning from high tide to low tide and back again. About twice a month, when the Earth, sun and moon are aligned at the new moon and full moon, we see more extreme tides rising higher (spring tide) and ebbing lower (neap tide).

And now the million-dollar question: if an adult human is about 60% water, what effect will those tidal pulls have on our body? It could be argued that there is no effect at all, since there is no measurable difference between the moon's gravitational pull on one side of our body compared to the other. Even in a big lake, the tides are still relatively minor. For example, the National Oceanic and Atmospheric Administration (NOAA) determined that tidal differences in the Great Lakes along the US border with Canada never exceed five centimetres, twice a day. Those minimal tidal shifts are almost undetectable, since they are drowned out by changes in wind and pressure that have a much bigger impact. For that reason, the lakes are considered non-tidal.

Still, that does not mean that we can completely discount the existence of these minimal tidal effects. The real question here is whether differences at the nano-scale can exert any significant influence. To answer that question, let's look at a study on *Arabadopsis thaliana* or thale cress conducted by the Max Planck Institute for Molecular Plant Physiology in Germany. It shows that the root growth of the plant seedling follows a cycle of 24.8 hours: exactly the time it takes for the moon to complete its pirouette around the Earth. The recorded effects involved minuscule changes that could only be measured with highly sensitive instruments, but the effects were definitely present. The scientists analysed the dynamics in clusters of water molecules within the plant cells and noted the day-to-day differences in the 'lunisolar gravity profile' caused by the moon's orbit and how these differences influence the volume of the water molecules. The movement of these molecular clusters within the roots and between cellular structures was affected by the direction of the lunisolar tidal force. The resulting oscillation in root elongation – the roots grew faster or slower in a cycle that correlated to the lunar day – could influence the entire organism, according to the study. And if plant cells are really that sensitive to tidal forces, the researchers at the Max Planck Institute do not see any reason why cells in the human body might not be similarly affected.

In addition, the tides would also have an effect on groundwater. Gardening in accordance with the phases of the moon is an ancient tradition, operating on the belief that the same gravitational pull that causes the tides will also make crops grow faster. As the moon pulls the ocean towards itself, it would also exert a gravitational pull on the groundwater; according to that reasoning, groundwater levels would also rise, enabling seeds to absorb more water at full moon. After that full moon, as the bright light and gravitational pull ebb away, the effects of the Earth's own gravity are felt more strongly, and the plants are rooted firmly in the soil.

In *The White Album*, Joan Didion writes about her visit to an orchid conservatory in Malibu, talking about how she had learned that the pollen

from one plant is carefully placed into the ovary of a flower on another, preferably at full moon and high tide, since moth orchids *(Phalaenopsis)* are supposedly more fertile then. The idea that *Phalaenopsis* plants were more fertile at full moon was based on the fact that the flowers are pollinated by nocturnal moths in nature. If you paid attention to our previous musings about moonlight, you understand why Didion writes that, over the course of 65 million years of evolution, periods of maximum fertility coincided with intervals of highest visibility. High tide is also said to influence orchid fertility; as lunar planters have always believed, moisture levels in plants work like the tides.

There in the greenhouse nothing would break the orchids and they would be pollinated at full moon and high tide by Amado Vasquez, and their seedlings would be tended in a sterile box with sterile gloves and sterile tools by Amado Vasquez's wife, Maria, and the orchids would not seem to die at all. 'We do not know how long they'll live,' Marvin Saltzman told me. 'They haven't been bred under protected conditions that long. The botanists estimate a hundred and fifty, two hundred years, but we don't know. All we know is that a plant a hundred years old will show no signs of senility.'

JOAN DIDION
The White Album

However, a host of other factors, from temperature to precipitation, do play a role in seed germination; as stated previously, it is not entirely clear whether the moon's gravitational pull has any significant impact on such biochemical processes. Still, the first human to plant a tiny seed in the soil must have looked up to the heavens for reassurance that it was the right time to plant – and if the harvest was satisfactory, that same human would have proclaimed with conviction: "The moon made me do it".

Northern Lights

Up on the roof, dancing for you under a million stars
Magnetic moon pulls me to you, with your ocean arms

TIFFANY
Magnetic Moon

As we said earlier, there have been studies that indicate changes in our sleep pattern throughout the lunar cycle. One such study conducted in a sleep lab in 2013 showed that it took the human subjects five minutes longer to fall asleep under the full moon, and that they slept 20 minutes less compared to the rest of the month. Brain activity was also monitored, which showed that deep sleep dropped by 30% – even if they were not actually exposed to the bright moonlight.

A follow-up study could not confirm these findings, but they do raise some questions. What could explain the influence on our sleep, if it was not moonlight? Could it still be that minimal gravitational pull? In any case, certain studies already link the impact of solar activity on the Earth's magnetic field to an increase in heart attacks and strokes, epilepsy, schizophrenia and suicide. The influence of solar flares and plasma clouds can lead to visible electric currents that are strong enough to cause electrical failures on Earth, and therefore could even affect electro-sensitive cells in the heart and brain.

The magnetic-moon theory is quite tempting to consider. Various studies also cite the importance of the CRY1 cryptochrome protein. The cryptochromes, which are sensitive to blue moonlight, not only play a role in the reproductive cycle of sexually excited corals; they are also the driving force in the circadian rhythms of plants and animals. In some species, such as fruit flies, the protein acts as a magnetic sensor. When cryptochromes bind themselves to flavin, a light-absorbing molecule, the circadian clock knows that it is daytime; in various species, including fruit flies, that photo-induced bond triggers a reaction that makes the molecular complex magnetically sensitive. Behavioural geneticists at the University of Leicester have shown that exposure to low-frequency electromagnetic fields can reset the circadian clocks of fruit flies *(Drosophila)*, which then changes their sleep pattern.

Although CRY1 also plays an important role in the human circadian clock, the protein works a little differently for us than for fruit flies. For instance, cryptochromes in humans and other mammals no longer bond with flavin; scientists are unsure how that form of magnetic sensitivity would develop without the essential flavin bond. Unless we have other molecules that make it possible to detect magnetic fields, cryptochromes seem unlikely to offer us an explanation.

This means that humans, unlike some birds, fishes and insects, traverse the Earth insensitive to those magnificent magnetic forces – although that assumption has been challenged by yet another study in which human subjects were exposed to magnetic fluctuations similar to what we would 'experience' when we travel locally. Their brain activity measurements showed a strong decrease in alpha waves. Our brains produce alpha waves when we are awake but idle, i.e. not engaged in any specific activity. Why this happens is not entirely clear. It could be an unimportant evolutionary side effect – or maybe magnetic changes in our environment do have a subtle influence on how our brains work?

There is still lots of room for scientific research on how the moon influences life on Earth. The possibilities seem endless; perhaps the only thing that is currently truly impossible is to definitively exclude any theories. Well, except the part about conceiving werewolves under the new moon. We're definitely not planning to put our sex lives on hold because of the 'dark side'.

A map of the moon

USE OF THE MOON

DISCOVER HOW YOU CAN USE THE MOON
IN YOUR DAILY LIFE

NEW MOON
Recharging

WAXING MOON
Getting started

●

FULL MOON
Apotheosis

❨

WANING MOON
Wrapping up

LUNAR CYCLES

HOW DO YOU MAKE THE MOST OF THE DIFFERENT LUNAR PHASES?

As the moon revolves around the Earth, sunlight shines on its surface from different angles. What we call moon cycles, lunar phases or phases of the moon are the different segments of the sunlit side of the moon that we can see from Earth. It takes about 29.5 days for the moon to revolve around the Earth, and each lunar phase lasts for approximately one week.

It's no coincidence that the word 'month' comes from the same roots as 'moon': the month was originally the interval between one new moon and the next. Although we no longer use a lunar calendar, as other cultures sometimes do, some people do use the lunar phase as a way to explain fluctuations in energy levels and mood.

Are you curious about how you can live more in sync with the rhythms of *la luna*? Then this is the chapter for you. As the moon swells and its light grows, our energy surges with it. Just as the moon moves in an elliptical orbit around the Earth, we ride the rollercoaster of life through its ups and downs, over and over, like the ebb and flow of the tide in response to the pull of the moon. The better prepared you are for these highs and lows, the less you'll need to fight against them, and the more you'll be able to simply lean back and enjoy the ride.

NEW MOON
Recharging

SCIENTIFIC

When the moon is on the same side as the sun, so the side facing us is not illuminated by the sun's rays, we call it a new moon. Don't worry; it's still the same old familiar friend, just a bit less 'in your face'. Historically, this lunar phase also used to be known as the 'dark side of the moon', since the Earth's satellite is not visible in the sky during this period ... although that's not quite correct, astronomically speaking (sorry, Pink Floyd!).

Since the moon's rotation around its axis takes just as long as its revolution around the Earth, she always shows the same face to the Earth, but the side that she doesn't show is only in complete darkness during the full moon. At all other times of the month, that hidden side is partly in sun and partly in shade. That's why astronomers refer to it as the 'far side' rather than the 'dark side'. Disappointed? You should know that the dividing line between the shaded and sunlit sides of the moon's surface is referred to by those same scientists as 'the lunar terminator'. Feel free to come up with your own clever wordplay involving the phases of the moon and 'I'll be back'.

SPIRITUAL

Unsurprisingly, the new moon is seen as a blank canvas, a new beginning, a fresh start, but above all it is seen as the time when you can take a moment to reflect and recentre yourself before embracing those new challenges. Reflect on what came before, relinquish negative thoughts, and recharge those internal batteries.

WHAT YOU CAN DO WITH IT

WELLNESS AND SELF-CARE

Historically, when most people lived in close proximity and menstrual cycles were more in sync, the new moon was when women would withdraw into private groups to have their period together. As cosy as that may sound, may we suggest a warm bath, a good book or a meditation session? This would also be a perfect moment to make a list of everything you were thankful for during the previous month. Thanks to the 'detox' levels of this phase of the moon – new moon, new me! – these three days can also be a great opportunity to cleanse yourself and your surroundings in every possible way. Going on a juice fast, doing seven loads of laundry on the highest settings, or shouting the name of your ex into a deep pit until you lose your voice: it's up to you. Use these days to head to bed on time and get up bright and early, so you're off to a good start for the rest of the month.

SEXUALITY AND RELATIONSHIPS

The nights are darker, and you can feel that lack of light in your energy levels and your desire for social contact. More accurately: your desire to avoid social contact at all costs. This isn't the right time to go out and party, but it's perfect for unplugging, being alone and taking it easy.

PROFESSIONAL LIFE

The new moon is a good time to reflect. Where are you right now in your career? What would you like to change? What steps would you need to take to get there? Listen to podcasts, watch TED Talks online, and absorb inspiration from your personal role models. As you feel your energy levels rising again and get your intellectual juices flowing, you can come up with a plan for the weeks ahead.

GARDENING

The new moon isn't the ideal time for sowing and planting, since it's too dark and the flows of energy are at their lowest ebb, but that doesn't mean there's nothing you can do in the garden. Plan your vegetable garden, prepare the soil, look at flowerpots online, and rotate your houseplants so their other sides will get more light in the next few weeks.

WAXING MOON
Getting started

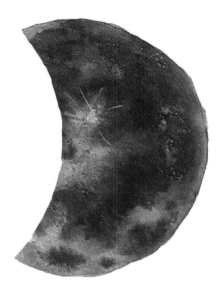

SCIENTIFIC

The side of the moon facing us sees more sunlight and forms a growing (or 'waxing') crescent on the right side. The waxing moon starts three days after the new moon and ends three days before the full moon. The halfway point of this phase is the half-moon, also known as the first quarter, since the moon is a quarter of the way through her cycle by that point. The angular separation between the sun and the moon is 90 degrees in this first quarter, so it visually resembles a semicircle. The second part of the waxing moon is the second quarter: from half-moon to full moon.

SPIRITUAL

Time to take action! All the plans you wrote down during the new moon can now be put into practice. This is the perfect time to grab opportunities, embrace new challenges, meet people or start a project. You'll see possibilities around every corner. As the moon's light grows night after night, you will also become more energetic, sociable and enterprising.

WHAT YOU CAN DO WITH IT

WELLNESS AND SELF-CARE

It takes several weeks to turn good intentions into good habits. When the waxing moon is in the sky, you'll see that you can stick to those good intentions just a little bit more easily. You're self-assured and confident. The waxing moon is a growing moon, and that growth also shines its light in the various aspects of your own life. During these days, it's easier to build muscle, so you should ideally focus on strength training. Since your hair will also grow faster, this is the perfect time to schedule an appointment with your hairdresser for a daring new haircut. Do be aware that many salons are closed on Mo(o)ndays.

SEXUALITY AND RELATIONSHIPS

Since the air is positively sizzling with good energy, this is when a first date will feel a little less scary, or you'll finally have the courage to let your crush know that you're alive and thinking of them. You can also test your limits in the bedroom. Interested in stepping outside your comfort zone, trying a new position, doing some light bondage or adding an exciting new location to your sex life? Go for it!

PROFESSIONAL LIFE

Let the waxing moon give you the courage to draw up a business plan, prepare a pitch or schedule a job interview: this is when you'll finally dare to answer honestly when they ask you how much money you're hoping to make. Your communication skills will be spot-on during the waxing moon, so make the most of that advantage.

GARDENING

The waxing moon is associated with growth, and you can take that pretty literally. People who have green fingers know for sure that this is a perfect time to sow and fertilise the soil, since there's more light even at night, and the moon's gravitational pull maximises the effect of the water in the soil. During the first few days of the waxing moon, it's best to plant fruit, vegetables and plants that grow above ground (like lettuce, spinach, cabbage, tomatoes, cucumbers, beans and melons), since the moon's pull is very strong, and the energy will flow upwards from the roots towards the leaves.

FULL MOON
Apotheosis

SCIENTIFIC

Two weeks after the new moon, our favourite satellite is halfway through its cycle and is now on the other side of the Earth, opposite the sun. That means that the side facing the Earth is bathed in sunlight, so the moon is a fully illuminated disc in the heavens above us. The full moon sets when the sun rises, and rises when the sun sets. The same thing happens during the new moon, but since it's almost completely dark then, you won't notice.

SPIRITUAL

The full moon brings out a lot of powerful emotions. Thanks to the mysterious presence of a bright sphere in the night sky, all sorts of special properties have been attributed to the full moon; some have even been researched by scientists on multiple occasions, as covered in the previous chapter. Generally, the full moon is assumed to be a time of climax. Everything peaks: your energy levels, your emotions, things that have been bubbling away under the surface for ages. Lots of people have reported insomnia during the full moon; some police officers say that violence, alcohol and drug use spike on those nights, and everyone simply seems to go a bit more ... lunatic.

WHAT YOU CAN DO WITH IT

WELLNESS AND SELF-CARE

It depends on how you feel right then and what you want to achieve. A full moon makes you braver and more energetic, creative and empathetic, but it boosts both good and bad emotions. Since a full moon brings out everyone's impulsive side, it's best to avoid signing contracts, making expensive purchases, or drastically changing your hairstyle during the three days surrounding the full moon.

SEXUALITY AND RELATIONSHIPS

Emotions are running high right now. This could be the night that you fly off the handle and pour out your suppressed frustrations to an unsuspecting colleague in a massive info-dump on WhatsApp, but it might just as easily be when you finally tell someone you love them. Since a full moon makes *everything* – yes, everything – more intense, it is a perfect time to have sex ... Even if you have to install Tinder to make it happen.

PROFESSIONAL LIFE

Conflicted. Some astrologers advise against signing contracts during a full moon, since you may feel so impulsive that you'll miss important details, while others argue that this is the perfect time for it. What they all agree on: if you're going to run into interesting details, opportunities that seem to come out of nowhere, or an unexpected contract offer, chances are good that it'll happen during the full moon.

GARDENING

If you have plants or flowers that are said to have special powers, this is the perfect time to check them out, because they'll be at maximum potential during the full moon. This isn't the time to sow or plant, but you can pick some healing herbs, make a herbal face mask, or try out a new recipe.

WANING MOON
Wrapping up

SCIENTIFIC

The waning moon is the exact opposite of the waxing moon: the full moon appears to gradually shrink, losing light from the right side until only a fingernail moon remains, in a crescent shape. The moon's light wanes in quarters, so the moon will look half-full again in the third quarter, having reached the three-quarters point in its loop around the Earth. Its light will continue to fade until the new moon or dark moon, when the cycle is complete.

SPIRITUAL

While the waxing moon causes energy to surge, you'll notice yourself growing calmer during the waning moon. That does not have to be negative. This often also means that you have more focus to finish current projects, let things go and gain some perspective. Some astrologers compare the moon's cycle to breathing. Inhale – growing and getting fresh air – during the waxing moon, and exhale symbolically during the waning moon.

WHAT YOU CAN DO WITH IT

WELLNESS AND SELF-CARE

Where the waxing moon represents increase or growth, the waning moon represents decrease or shrinkage. Astrologers will advise you that this is a good time to start a diet or sort through your stuff, finally taking those books to the second-hand shop or donating your winter jumpers to charity. Letting go can also be a mental process: this is a time to forgive people, or possibly even forget them. If you picked up good habits during the waxing moon, you can use the waning moon to get rid of some bad ones. If you're hoping to stop smoking or give up biting your nails, this time of the month will be your best bet.

SEXUALITY AND RELATIONSHIPS

After the intensity of the full moon, you'll feel satiated, calmer, less restless. This is a period in which many people feel a strong sense of love and gratitude for those around them, so it's a perfect time to treat your partner to a massage or invite your friends over for dinner.

PROFESSIONAL LIFE

Now is not the time for wild schemes or grand business meetings, but it is a great chance to work through piles of (monotonous) projects. You may feel less creative, but your perseverance will keep your chin up and your days productive. This is also when you can clean up your desk, catch up on answering emails, do your admin or – however sadly – let those employees go.

GARDENING

In the world of plants, gardeners recommend harvesting and weeding during the waning moon. This would also be the right time to mow your grass, since it's said to grow more slowly during this period. Do you have seedlings that still need to be thinned out? The waning moon is the time to do it. In your vegetable garden, you should be focusing on plants growing mainly underground right now (like onions, beets, carrots and potatoes), since the moon's pull is in decline and energy is flowing downwards in this lunar phase.

Do not swear by the moon,
for she changes constantly
then your love would also change

WILLIAM SHAKESPEARE

OTHER
MOON PHENOMENA

WHAT IS A BLUE MOON, A BLOOD MOON
AND A SUPER MOON?

SUPERMOON

We're not easily satisfied, as is apparent from the concept of the 'supermoon'. That term is used when the moon swings closer to the Earth, making it look larger and brighter. The moon's orbit isn't a perfect circle; it moves in an ellipse around the Earth, so the distance between the moon and the Earth varies between about 357,000 km and 406,000 km. When the moon's orbit brings it closest to the Earth, it's just 356,400 km away. At that distance, its perceived diameter is nearly 14% larger than usual, and the moon looks about 30% brighter than normal. However, the difference is hardly visible to the naked eye. Would you like to enjoy the full glory of that extra *oomph*? Turn to page 143 to read about how you can build your own telescope.

LUNAR ECLIPSE

When our planet is precisely aligned with the moon and the sun, and the moon and the sun are on opposite sides of the Earth with us in the middle, the Earth's shadow blocks the sunlight from hitting the moon. This is known as a lunar eclipse. Since the moon's orbit around the Earth is tilted about 5 degrees from the plane on which the Earth revolves around the sun, a lunar eclipse is not very common; it only occurs when the moon is at the node where the orbital planes intersect. Unlike a solar eclipse, which occurs when the moon is between the sun and the Earth, and is only visible for a few minutes from specific places on the Earth's surface when it occurs, a lunar eclipse can be viewed from anywhere on Earth – but only at night.

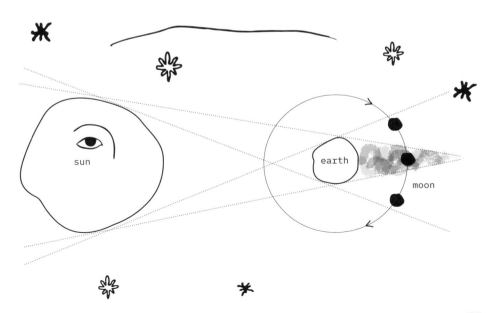

BLOOD MOON

Contrary to what you might expect, the moon is not completely dark during a lunar eclipse. The sunlight that passes by the Earth and hits the moon is reflected back to the Earth as reddish light due to the composition of our atmosphere, giving the moon a brownish-red glow. Colloquially, this is known as a 'blood moon'. Dramatic-sounding, isn't it? The intensity of the red colour depends on the amount of dust in the atmosphere: a bright red moon means lots of dust in the air.

BLUE MOON

A lunar cycle takes about 29.5 days, but the months on our calendar vary between 28 and 31 days. That means that the full moon sometimes happens twice within the same month, and the second full moon in a month is known as a 'blue moon'. It's not all that unusual, by the way. Astronomers estimate that there's a blue moon in our skies every 2.7 years, although the name shouldn't be taken too literally: unlike the blood moon, the blue moon doesn't actually turn indigo. Its name has nothing to do with its colour, but with the English expression for a rare occurrence: 'once in a blue moon'.

But isn't that backwards, to have the phenomenon referring to the expression? Nope! Folklorist Philip Hiscock says that the concept of the 'blue moon' has been around for more than 400 years, but the astronomical phenomenon only entered into common usage about thirty years ago. Originally, 'blue moon' was synonymous with 'never': 'I'll marry you when the moon turns blue'. From there, it gradually evolved into the expression we use today.

Separate from any calendar events, the moon may sometimes appear blue. The ash and soot in the air after a volcanic eruption or forest fire may filter colours, adding a greenish-blue tinge to sunsets and moonlight.

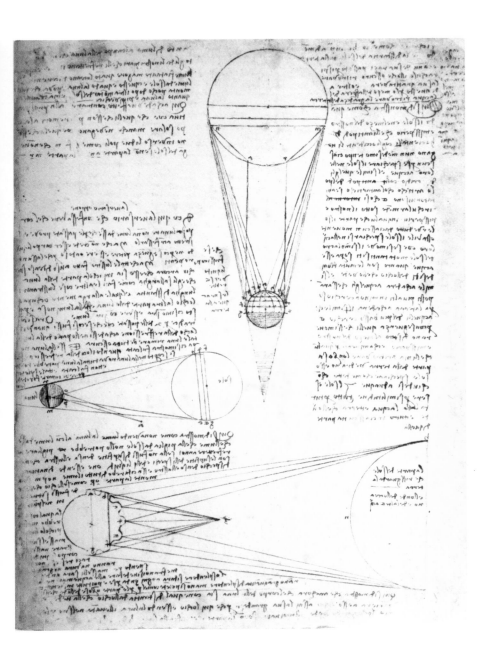

Moon Sketch by Leonardo Da Vinci

MOON RITUALS

FROM MOON-BATHING TO SMUDGING

'MOON-BATHING'

In Ayurvedic practice, a system of alternative medicine with its roots in India, moon-bathing is used to cool down excess *pitta dosha*. The moonlight's *yin* nature counterbalances the *yang* of the sun's rays, which overheat our body, metabolism and temperament. The artificial light from our computer screens, the fluorescent lighting in our offices and the constant glow of our smartphones all feed into the fiery energy of the *pitta dosha*. Moon-bathing is said to be beneficial for rashes, infections and high blood pressure, although there is no scientific evidence to support these claims.

There are various ways to go 'moon-bathing', but it's supposed to be most effective in the period between new moon and full moon. Die-hard yogis practice moon-bathing by sitting in a moonlit room (or an open field), surrounded by bowls of water that – according to their beliefs – collect the energies of the moonlight, which is then used for bathing or drinking. Generally speaking, the point is to come into contact with moonlight, for example by going on an evening stroll after dark, sitting by the window in a pool of moonlight, or – just like sun-bathing – flat on your back in the open air while lying on a beach towel.

'MOON-BREATHING'

All right, moon-breathing doesn't actually involve the moon at all, except for its name, but the yogic breathing exercise has so many benefits that you absolutely need to know about it. Moon-breathing is associated with *kaizen*, the Japanese concept of iterative improvement based on performing daily routines optimally, and thus gradually improving your life. *Chandra bheda-na pranayama* or 'moon-piercing breath' is a breathing exercise intended to calm you down, and can be performed while sitting at your desk or lying in bed at home. Moon-breathing involves inhaling through your left nostril only, since the left side of the body is associated with the nervous system, and exhaling through your right nostril only. The exercise has traditionally been used to induce calm, relaxation and deep sleep.

HOW TO DO MOON-BREATHING

Use your right thumb to close your right nostril. Let the first finger and middle finger of your right hand (the same hand) rest gently on your palm, while extending your ring finger and little finger. Now inhale slowly and deeply through your unobstructed left nostril.

Then use the ring finger of your right hand to pinch your left nostril closed, and lift your thumb from your right nostril so you can exhale from the right. Repeat this breathing exercise several times until you feel yourself slipping into a state of relaxation.

SMUDGING

Smudging is a technique for using smoke to 'cleanse' a room and invite positive energy into the space. The practice is common amongst various indigenous peoples of North and South America, and similar customs are used in Buddhism. It involves burning a small bundle of (dried) plants and herbs, allowing the smoke to fill the room to cleanse it. Smudging is often done during the new moon, since this is the ideal time for a fresh start.

HERE'S HOW TO MAKE YOUR OWN SMUDGE STICK

Gather herbs and hang them upside down to dry. Different herbs have different meanings, so you can design your smudge stick based on what you want to do with it. The most popular herbs and plants for a smudge stick are white sage, lavender, juniper, mugwort, cedar leaf and rosemary. If you don't have these plants in your own garden, check out your local farmer's market or post a request in a gardening group on Facebook: they'll definitely be able to help you. Once the herbs are dried, you can tie them together using a piece of plain, undyed twine or thread; wrap it around the herbs to hold the stems and leaves in a neat little bundle, forming a smudge stick.

HERE'S HOW TO SMUDGE YOUR HOUSE

Start at the front door and light your smudge stick using a candle, match or lighter. The tip should start to smoulder and smoke. From the front door, move clockwise through all the spaces of the house, making sure that the smoke creeps into every little corner. Don't worry, it won't produce enough smoke to set off your smoke detectors and disturb the restored calm before you're even finished! As you move through your house, make sure to think positive thoughts and imagine what you want from each room. In the bedroom, you could think about a solid night's rest or a satisfying orgasm; in the kitchen, set your mind to healthy meals; in the bathroom, contemplate trying to stop picking at your spots. When you're finished, don't forget to carefully extinguish your smudge stick in a bowl of sand – not in your kitchen sink!

my moon, my man
so changeable and
such a loveable lamb to me

my moon's white face
what day and what phase
it's the calendar page again.

FEIST
My Moon, My Man

MOON-GAZING FOR BEGINNERS

WHAT, WHERE AND WHEN IS THE BEST WAY OF LOOKING AT THE MOON?

What's your first memory of the moon? Close your eyes for a moment and try to recall. For us, Wallace and Gromit make a surprise appearance, heading off to hunt cheese on the moon. Or the actual moon on holiday, teensy-tiny and soaring high above the horizon in the dark night sky. The red telescope that we secretly snuck out from under our brother's bed for a few minutes to glimpse a different view of the moon for five seconds. Or the solar eclipse in summer 1998 and those protective goggles that were handed out weeks beforehand. Two dark minutes on our way home from the supermarket. We didn't see the sun, but the moon that had come between us.

Later, when we were grown, we started actively seeking out the moon. Setting our alarms to run down to the parking lot in our pyjamas and stare at a disc drenched in red. Hoping that the drunk party-goers just heading home would look up from the ground for a moment – the sight would be more than worth the fall. And besides, when you're lying in the gutter, you're looking at the stars. That's what Oscar Wilde said.

Maybe it doesn't matter much where you are. Whether you're in a forest, on the beach or on the pavement outside a nightclub surrounded by glittering city lights: the moon will always be there, and it will always be different. But if the moon works so hard to show off its best side every time we look up, why not broaden our perspective? Once you know how to look at the moon, you'll never get tired of seeing it.

WHAT YOU NEED

1. BINOCULARS OR A TELESCOPE

You don't have to invest in a serious telescope if you don't want to go overboard on moon-gazing, or don't want to eat nothing but ramen noodles for the rest of the month. Binoculars will get you pretty far already; you'll actually be able to see the same level of detail that Galileo saw when he peered at the sky through the first telescope – so that includes Jupiter's four largest moons, which he discovered in 1610! (They're now known as the Galilean satellites: Io, Europa, Ganymede and Callisto.) Even if you just stick to our own planetary satellite, you can spend delightful hours tracing the topographical lines of mountains, plains and craters.

It's no easy task to hold a pair of binoculars perfectly still. The slightest movement will cause the image to swoop and shift, which isn't ideal when you're moon-gazing. For an easier peek, you can opt for binoculars that include image stabilisation, although they will be a bit more expensive. You can also use what you find around you: stabilise your binoculars on a wall or against a tree, or rest your elbows on the ground or your chair, holding the binoculars firmly to your eyes.

If you really want to take it to the next level, you can discover more hidden features of the moon with a small telescope. In general, you can get a maximum magnification of 50x per 25 mm. If you have an objective lens of 100 mm, it's best not to go above 200x magnification: since you're basically just magnifying the natural conditions of the night sky, too much zoom will generally lead to a darker image that's super shaky.

2. A MAP OF THE MOON

When you head out to explore a new city or neighbourhood, you usually open Google Maps on your phone. We should check out a map of the moon just as easily and automatically as we do in our earthly wanderings. To identify the major landmarks more easily, look at a good map of the moon beside

143

a clear photo of the lunar surface. The NASA space probe known as the Lunar Reconnaissance Orbiter (LRO) gave us beautiful images and maps of the craters and plains across the lunar landscape.

An average map shows the moon as you would see it in the sky with the naked eye: northwards is up. Make sure you check what you're seeing through your binoculars or telescope. Sometimes the image is rotated 180 degrees, or even reversed. If that is the case, you'll need to rotate the map as well, or flip it around in your mind.

3. A NOTEBOOK

Throughout our history, various cultures have developed widely diverse stories about the shapes we can see in the moon. Some see rabbits hopping across the silvery landscape, while others see a dog, a man, a lizard, a frog, a crab or a woman knitting. Now that you're gazing up at the moon with binoculars or a telescope, you may see something else entirely. You can note down all these first impressions in your personal notebook of observations. Definitely don't forget to make a note of the date and time, and the instrument you used for the observation. This will help you build up a nice logbook that you can page through nostalgically later on: the falling star that arched over the moon, the wish you made, the first snow under the blood moon's glow, the perfect hillside under a clear stretch of night sky.

4. A COMFORTABLE CHAIR

You're following these step-by-step instructions so you can admire the moon in greater detail. It would be a shame to miss the little details because you can't concentrate. Few things are more distracting than developing muscle cramps or getting chilled while moon-gazing. Check the weather report and dress for the forecast, and make sure you have a comfortable chair and good posture, because it's going to be a long night.

HERE'S HOW TO MAKE YOUR OWN TELESCOPE

The basics

- Two converging lenses that are about 2–3 cm in diameter.
  One is larger than the other
- Two cardboard tubes that can slide into each other,
  like the tubes from toilet paper or aluminium foil
- A thick sheet of paper or cardboard
- Black paint and a paintbrush
- Star stickers
- Black tape and glue
- Scissors or a hobby knife
- A measuring tape or ruler

Instructions

1. Apply black paint to both cardboard tubes and the sheet of paper
   or cardboard. Let the paint dry.

2. The two tubes will form the basic structure of your telescope. Add
   up the focal length of the two lenses, divide that number by two,
   and then add 2.5 cm: this will be the length of each tube. Use your
   scissors or hobby knife to cut the tubes to the right length and
   slide the narrower tube inside the wider tube.

3. Measure the diameter of the smaller tube and cut a disc of the
   same diameter from the sheet of thick paper or cardboard. Cut
   out the middle of the disc, removing a circle that is slightly smaller
   in diameter than the smaller lens. Glue the lens onto the opening.
   Do the same for the larger tube and the larger lens.

4. Finally, using glue and/or tape, attach the small disc to the end of
   the small tube to look through, and attach the larger disc to the
   end of the larger tube.

5. Put star stickers all over the outside of your telescope.

6. Look through the eyepiece and point your telescope at the night
   sky. Adjust the picture by sliding the tubes in and out until the
   image is in focus. What do you see?

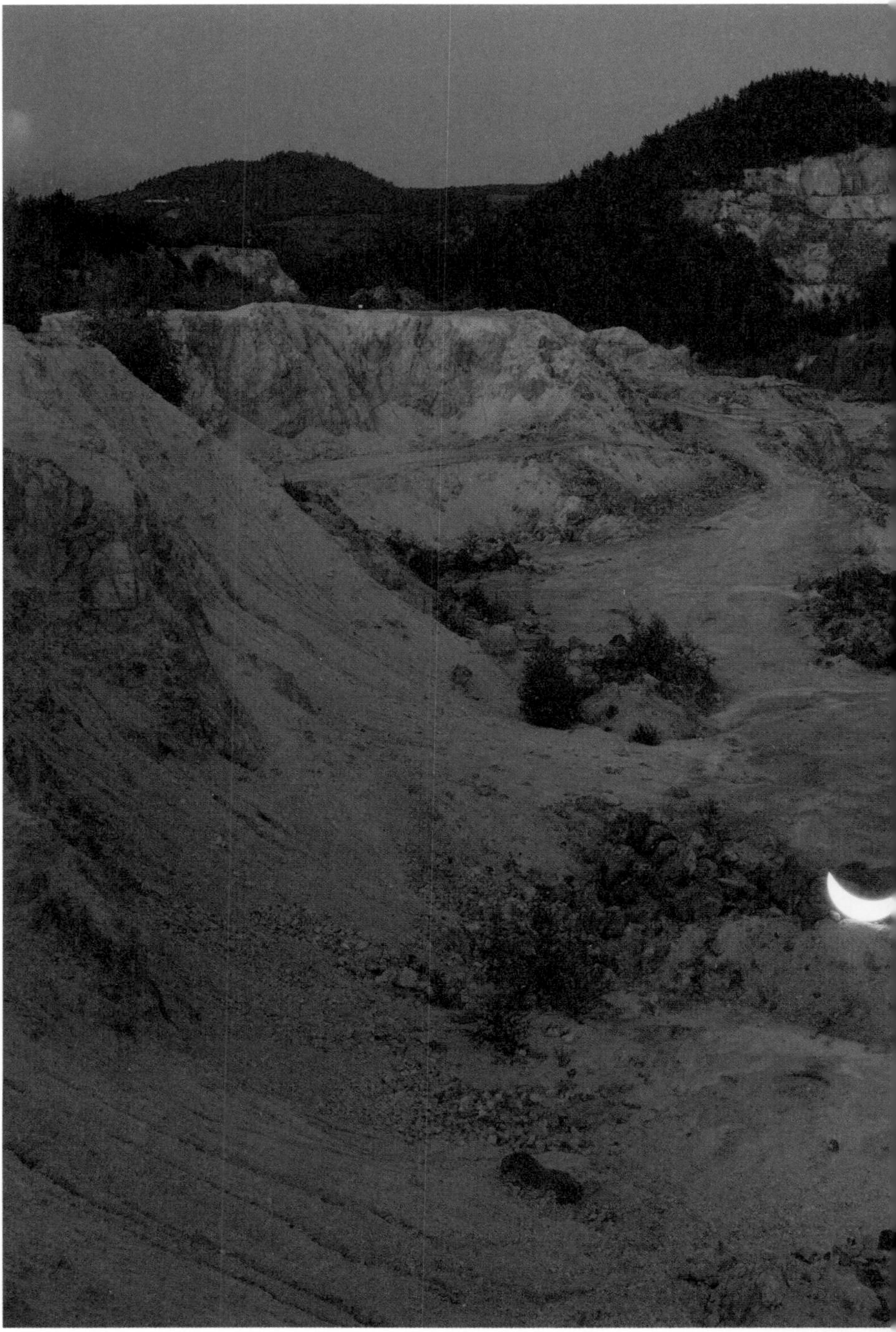

WHEN TO LOOK AT THE SKY

Basically, you can start directing your gaze towards the heavens in the first days after the new moon. That's when the crescent sliver can be seen in the western skies at night. At that point, the slender curve only shows us *Mare Crisium*, but the light reflected by the Earth casts a mystical glow that reveals the shadow side of the moon in our sights.

If you're hoping to see more, just wait a few more days. The lunar terminator (the line separating day from night on the moon) will slowly move across the disc, revealing more details. We see the moon swell through its first quarter (the half-moon) into the waxing moon, climaxing in the blindingly bright full moon.

The best time to look at the moon is in the first quarter and the days right after that, or the final quarter and the days just before that, especially if you're taking a closer look at the lunar landscape along the terminator. During those periods, the moon is ideally illuminated: not too little, not too much. In its first quarter, the moon is at exactly 50%, which is only an eleventh as bright as its gleam at full brightness. That is because the half-moon is still awash in shadows, even on its illuminated side. Two to four days before the full moon, we basically see it shining only half as brightly.

However, as the terminator slides farther across the moon and the sun climbs higher, the shadows shrink, and the contours of the lunar landscape seem to melt away. In other words, the full moon appears relatively flat, and the minimal shadows can also seem – literally – blinding through the lens of your binoculars or telescope. A lunar filter for your professional telescope can reduce that glare long enough to reveal more details, allowing you to enjoy the magnificent moon in all its phases.

MOON FACT
Imagine the moon for a moment. You were probably envisioning a crescent or a circle. Despite that default, we see the waxing moon much more frequently over the course of our lives – although it is often mistaken for the full moon in its final days. Where the young crescent moon only allows us a brief glimpse in the early hours of the morning and evening, the waxing moon can be seen in the sky for over half the night, and is also visible during the day. And it can be seen for half a month, between the first and last quarter.

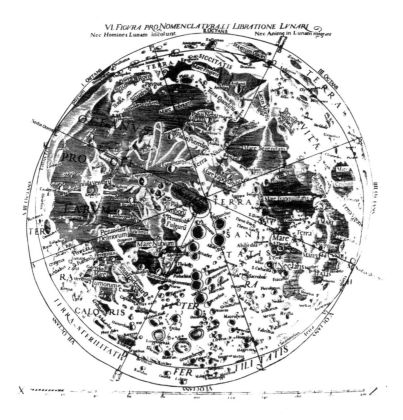

A 17th Century map of the moon

WHAT YOU WILL SEE

MOUNTAINS

The Apennines. The Caucasus. The Pyrenees. Not the mountains we know so well here on Earth, but their mysterious lunar equivalents that share the same names. Take an especially close look at the zones along the lunar terminator. In the twilight along the terminator, the low-hanging sun casts longer shadows, showing the moon's hills and valleys in sharp contrast and making them more clearly visible.

SEAS

The dark grey spots that you see in the moon are called the lunar maria; *maria* is the plural form of *mare*, the Latin word for sea, because we once thought that there was water on the moon. Back in the 17th century, Italian astronomer Giambattista Riccioli gave those illusory oceans such elegant names as *Mare Serenitatis* ('Sea of Serenity') and *Sinus Iridum* ('Bay of Rainbows'). By now, we have learned that the moon is bone-dry, and that the lunar maria are actually flat plains created 3.5 billion years ago when asteroids hit the moon, forming craters that filled up with lava pushing upwards from beneath the lunar crust. Even so, there is no harm in retaining the poetic names of the seas that appear in sequence throughout the various lunar phases: *Mare Tranquilitatis, Serenitatis, Imbrium*, and finally *Oceanus* and *Procellarum*.

CRATERS

Nestled between the maria, the stark white highlands are much older, pockmarked by thousands of craters. If you point your binoculars or telescope at the lunar terminator a few days after the half-moon, you will see the crater Copernicus appear in your sights. Obviously, the crater was named after the man who came up with the heliocentric concept of the solar system: Nicholas Copernicus. The prominent ray system of the impact crater extends 400 km

beyond its edges, in a pattern reminiscent of the sun's own rays. Another well-known crater is Tycho, named after Danish astronomer Tycho Brahe. This crater also has long white lines radiating hundreds of kilometres across the lunar landscape: the largest ray system on our planet's satellite. If you have keen eyesight, you could even try to see the Tycho ray system without binoculars.

NOT DONE SKYGAZING YET?

If you just can't get enough of moon-gazing, you can literally expand your horizons and look farther to the four moons of Jupiter. Io, Europa, Ganymede and Callisto can be viewed from the Earth using a telescope. For a real challenge, you can try to track them down with binoculars. Once you locate the bright planet in the night sky, you'll see four glittering dots nearby. If you observe them for several weeks in a row, you'll see how the positions of the Galilean satellites shift night after night. That's because each of the moons follows its own orbit around Jupiter. If you went ahead and got that telescope, you'd also be able to admire Saturn's marvels – not only its rings and its regal golden colour, but also the planet's biggest moon: Titan.

WHERE TO BE

On International Observe the Moon Night, a NASA initiative launched in 2010, the whole world looks up at the moon. If you would like to take part in one of the upcoming events on 26 September 2020, 16 October 2021, or 1 October 2022, you'll want to go to the best possible location. That means far away from any cities, with clear skies and maximum darkness. That's far from easy, if you realise that about two-thirds of the world's population is shrouded in the glow of light pollution. As a result, the most breathtaking locations are quite remote and difficult to reach. Still worth it, though, because nothing is more satisfying then the rewards that took extra effort to achieve, right?

DESERTS

Large desert regions are generally mostly uninhabited, so light pollution is much less of a problem there. Moreover, such extremely dry areas are likely to have clear night skies. In other words, the desert is an ideal destination for moon-gazers. The scorching Sahara, which covers about 10% of the African continent, offers some of the most spectacular starry skies. We saw it for ourselves: a brief nighttime expedition into the Moroccan Sahara, coincidentally accompanied by an astrophysicist from Cambridge, convinced us to abandon the Skyview app (although it had been handy up to then). Upon seeing all that dazzling beauty in a dark vacuum, we wept uncontrollably, almost enough to fill a river flowing through that arid landscape.

In the Namib Desert, similar conditions create the perfect setting for moon-gazing. In fact, it's even better: the vast desert of Namibia is completely flat, so you can enjoy 360° views of the night sky. No wonder Namibia has become a hugely popular destination for astronomy tourists.

Finally, if you'd like to imagine what it would be like on Mars and see pretty much the best view of the universe in the southern hemisphere, you can go to the Atacama Desert. Stretching across Chile and small parts of Peru, Bolivia and Argentina, the red desert is situated at an altitude of 4,000 m and is the driest desert in the world, receiving only 1 mm of rainfall a year ... and ensuring very clear skies at night. Observatories are scattered all across the Atacama Desert, offering a peek at the minute details of the universe; the Paranal Observatory has one of the biggest telescopes in the world.

FROM GREAT HEIGHTS

It was in the gorgeous rolling hills of Tuscany that Galileo developed his telescope and first directed it towards the heavens. Obviously, the Tuscan countryside had to be included on our list. However, if you'd like to visit one of the last places in Western Europe to glimpse the natural night skies, you'll have to head a bit farther north, into the Alps. Why not integrate a session of moon-gazing into your après-ski party?

You could also set even higher standards ... literally. The Himalayas are the highest mountain range in the world, with Mount Everest soaring about 8,850 m above sea level. The crystal-clear skies make these mountain peaks a perfect spot to pull out your binoculars and look up.

To bring the theme to a close from greater heights, we travelled to Lake Titicaca, a huge body of water on the border between Peru and Bolivia. At an elevation of 3,812 m, you'll be a lot closer to the moon. When the skies are clear, you won't even need binoculars or a telescope. To behold all the moon's beauty, you'll only need your own two eyes; the universe will do the rest.

VOLCANOES

The Canary Islands feature seven different volcanoes, offering an excellent destination for moon-gazers. No wonder it's home to the world's biggest telescope, bearing the very original name of Gran Telescopio de Canarias. The gorgeous silver structure rises 12 stories into the air. La Palma is popular among astronomy tourists, and was even designated a UNESCO biosphere reserve in 2002. Tenerife – widely known for relaxing besides holidays – is also a great place to go.

Although Hawaii might evoke impressions of sunbathing on sandy beaches (and we can't deny that you also see wonderfully starry night skies on those islands as well), it's the tall volcanoes that catapulted Hawaii towards the top of our list. Mauna Kea and Mauna Loa are both more than 4,000 m above sea level and are known for their absolutely amazing views of the universe.

NATIONAL PARKS

Nature reserves and national parks are protected areas, so they are usually exempted from serious light pollution. From Death Valley to Bryce Canyon: these national parks across the USA are dark paradises where the falling stars spin through heaven like silken thread and nothing can distract you from the moon's full glory.

The Australian outback is another good place to seek out the darkest nights. Moreover, the night skies in the southern hemisphere are even more beautiful to behold than in the northern regions: you can see the bright core of the Milky Way galaxy dancing above your head.

The stated mission of the International Dark Sky Association (IDA) is to protect dark skies all around the world. In August 2019, the IDA designated over 120 locations worldwide, including a number of IDA International Dark Sky Park (IDSP) sites: areas with exceptionally starry night skies and a night-time setting which is protected for its scientific, nature-oriented, educational, cultural and public value. If you're planning a trip: we've listed the designated parks below, and maybe you can use the overview of these IDA parks at the end of the book as a bucket list?

MOON HOROSCOPE

CALCULATE YOUR MOON SIGN
AND LEARN WHAT THAT MEANS

We all know our star sign: the astrological sign in which the most famous star (our own sun) stood at the moment of our birth. To some extent,
the star sign describes our personality – but only partly, because we not only
have a star sign (based on the position of the sun) but also a moon sign,
based on where the moon was when we were born.

Everyone can easily figure out their star sign based on the day and
month in which they were born, since the sun progresses steadily through
the constellations that make up the zodiac signs, spending about one month
in each sign. The moon moves much faster across the sky, spending about
two and a quarter days in each sign, but also moving in a different pattern
than the sun. As a result, your moon sign isn't all that easy to calculate; you'll
need to figure out the exact position of the moon at the moment you entered
the world. You can work it out yourself using the tables below, or get some
astrological assistance from apps and websites (see page 189) that will calculate your moon sign in just a few seconds.

HOW TO CALCULATE YOUR MOON SIGN

Step 1
In the first table, look up your birth year and see where the moon was on the first day of the month in which you were born.

Step 2
In the second table, look up how many zodiac signs you need to move forward based on the third table.

Example
Katrin Swartenbroux was born on 29 November 1986.
In 1986 the moon was in Libra on 1 November.
The 29th day means moving forward one zodiac sign, so Katrin's moon sign is Scorpio.

Please note
This method is reasonably accurate, but your birthday may fall on a day in which the moon moves from one zodiac sign to the next, in which case your moon sign would depend on the hour in which you were born.

If the description doesn't sound familiar to you, check the sign before or after your estimate to see if that fits you better. Only an experienced astrologer (or an app) can calculate your exact birth chart, including your exact moon sign.

All right, but why is it so important to know your moon sign? Have you ever read the description of your zodiac sign and thought: what, no! What kind of nonsense is this charlatan spouting? What do you mean, I'm bossy? I'm incredibly shy and insecure! That's logical, because your star sign is only one factor in your birth chart. To get a really clear analysis of your astrological composition, you need to know the position of all the planets and satellites at the moment of your birth.

TABLE 1

Moon sign tables for the years 1950–2050

AR OF BIRTH						JAN	FEB	MAR	APR	MAY	JUN	JUL	AUG	SEPT	OCT	NOV	DEC
50	1969	1988	2007	2026	2045	TAU	CAN	CAN	VIR	LIB	SAG	CAP	PIS	ARI	GEM	CAN	LEO
51	1970	1989	2008	2027	2046	LIB	SAG	SAG	AQU	PIS	TAU	GEM	CAN	VIR	LIB	SAG	CAP
52	1971	1990	2009	2028	2047	PIS	ARI	TAU	GEM	CAN	VIR	LIB	SAG	CAP	AQU	ARI	TAU
53	1972	1991	2010	2029	2048	CAN	VIR	VIR	LIB	SAG	CAP	PIS	ARI	GEM	CAN	VIR	LIB
54	1973	1992	2011	2030	2049	SCO	CAP	CAP	PIS	ARI	GEM	CAN	VIR	SCO	SAG	CAP	AQU
55	1974	1993	2012	2031	2050	ARI	TAU	GEM	LEO	VIR	LIB	SCO	CAP	PIS	ARI	TAU	CAN
56	1975	1994	2013	2032		LEO	LIB	LIB	SAG	CAP	PIS	ARI	TAU	CAN	LEO	LIB	SCO
57	1976	1995	2014	2033		CAP	AQU	PIS	ARI	TAU	CAN	LEO	LIB	SCO	CAP	AQU	ARI
58	1977	1996	2015	2034		TAU	CAN	CAN	VIR	LIB	SAG	CAP	AQU	ARI	TAU	CAN	LEO
59	1978	1997	2016	2035		LIB	SCO	SAG	CAP	AQU	ARI	TAU	CAN	LEO	VIR	SCO	SAG
60	1979	1998	2017	2036		AQU	ARI	ARI	GEM	CAN	LEO	VIR	SCO	CAP	AQU	ARI	TAU
61	1980	1999	2018	2037		GEM	LEO	LEO	LIB	SCO	CAP	AQU	ARI	TAU	GEM	LEO	VIR
62	1981	2000	2019	2038		SCO	SAG	CAP	AQU	ARI	TAU	GEM	LEO	LIB	SCO	SAG	SAG
63	1982	2001	2020	2039		PIS	TAU	TAU	CAN	LEO	LIB	SCO	SAG	AQU	PIS	TAU	GEM
64	1983	2002	2021	2040		LEO	VIR	LIB	SCO	SAG	AQU	PIS	TAU	CAN	LEO	VIR	LIB
65	1984	2003	2022	2041		SAG	CAP	AQU	PIS	TAU	GEM	LEO	VIR	SCO	SAG	AQU	PIS
66	1985	2004	2023	2042		ARI	GEM	GEM	LEO	VIR	SCO	SAG	AQU	PIS	ARI	GEM	CAN
67	1986	2005	2024	2043		VIR	SCO	SCO	CAP	AQU	PIS	TAU	GEM	LEO	VIR	LIB	SAG
68	1987	2006	2025	2044		CAP	PIS	PIS	TAU	GEM	LEO	VIR	SCO	SAG	CAP	PIS	ARI

TABLE 2

number of signs to be added for each day of the month

DAY	ADD (SIGNS)	DAY	ADD (SIGNS)
1	0	16	7
2	1	17	7
3	1	18	8
4	1	19	8
5	2	20	9
6	2	21	9
7	3	22	10
8	3	23	10
9	4	24	10
10	4	25	11
11	5	26	11
12	5	27	12
13	5	28	12
14	6	29	1
15	6	30	1
		31	2

TABLE 3

signs of the zodiac

1	Aries (ARI)
2	Taurus (TAU)
3	Gemini (GEM)
4	Cancer (CAN)
5	Leo (LEO)
6	Virgo (VIR)
7	Libra (LIB)
8	Scorpio (SCO)
9	Sagittarius (SAG)
10	Capricorn (CAP)
11	Aquarius (AQU)
12	Pisces (PIS)

Where your zodiac sign or 'sun sign' describes how you project yourself to the world outside (and how people see you), your moon sign determines your inner self: how you see yourself, how you feel, how you deal with emotions, and how your subconscious works. Where your sun sign is what you apparently project to others, your moon sign encompasses your deepest self. That's why it can be useful to know your moon sign (and the moon signs of your best friends or partner).

In the following section, you will read about how the various moon signs work, and which signs they are most compatible with.

ARIES

It's unsurprising that your stormy nature is embodied by a horned animal that rushes at everything headlong. You are fierce, which can be both positive and negative. You are enthusiastic, dynamic and spontaneous, but also irritable, easily bored and impatient.

People with Aries as their moon sign have a short fuse and are unafraid to embrace confrontation, but also find it easy to forgive and forget. You're the type to tumble head over heels into relationships, and decide just as quickly that it's not working out after all. If your partner needs a bit more time to process it all, you'll have a hard time understanding why.

You're a go-getter and will always pursue success, in your professional life, sports or in relationships. However, your impetuous nature may be startling or off-putting to others. The person who suddenly wipes the whiteboard clean in the middle of the meeting and exclaims: let's go brainstorm outside? Check. The lover who suggests the butt plugs on the third date? Check check. The occasional jogger who decides one morning to run a marathon later that year, and then actually does it? Check check check.

Long story short, you always know what you want, and you go for it 100%, but what you want might change from day to day. Not exhausting at all, really.

TAURUS

You might not think it, but people who have their moon in the Taurus constellation are incredibly cautious. The bull. Cautious. That's right. In relationships, money and work, you opt for stability. You enjoy measuring your wealth based on material possessions and love luxury, but you'll never make an impulsive purchase casually. Your practical mindset makes it likely that you drive a well-made car that isn't particularly cheap, and have a special cover that you pull over it when you have to use street parking.

You may initially come across as reserved, possibly even a little cold, but anyone who really knows you would describe you as a warm, hospitable person. It's not easy to win the heart of someone with their moon in Taurus, but once someone's gained your trust, you will be one of the most caring, loyal companions that anyone could wish for. One-night stands are absolutely not your thing, and improv comedy is your worst nightmare. You're not guided by your fear, but you are a creature of habit: the type of person who always opts for the same dish in the same restaurant, and occasionally orders a different aperitif when you really want to 'go wild'.

That also makes you emotionally stable, although you may tend to be a bit suspicious, since your deep-seated need for security takes precedence. You need lots of validation, but that's okay. Really.

GEMINI

This could go two ways: Either you toss this book aside after reading the Gemini description (setting it on fire would be too dramatic for you), or you underline the quote and share it on all your social media accounts for your thousands of followers. You're an exceptionally communicative person, willing to share your opinions and insights with anyone who wants to hear them – and yes, also with everyone else. You're constantly in dialogue, but tend to surround yourself with like-minded people, so your world is a bit of an echo chamber.

People with their moon in Gemini have a short attention span, but aren't particularly impulsive as a result. You offer sensitive input and need lots of intellectual stimulation, but view each new experience through the lens of logic. That makes it easy for you to learn new things, so you excel at every fleeting hobby that you pick up and then set aside again.

Have we already mentioned that you tend to be social? You're social. Very social. You're an incorrigible flirt with a need for freedom who's constantly looking for a good conversation. Contradictorily, you may initially seem a bit superficial, because it's hard for people to get really close to you. Fair's fair: in combination with your clever comments and quick mind, that can be quite intriguing.

PS: Please tag us when you share this on Instagram.

CANCER

That protective shell that encloses the crab? You have that too, at least figuratively (hopefully not literally!). You are quick to build high walls around yourself and protect your way of thinking – and it happens regularly, because you're also quick to go on the defensive. And maybe, just maybe, you might not be all that awesome at expressing things in nuanced ways. At the same time, you are incredibly empathetic and intuitive, so you're probably completely right when you worry that one of your friends is being fooled by someone doesn't have her best interests in mind, again.

Once that happens, the culprit will never be able to get into your good graces again: you believe that everyone deserves a second chance, but anyone who hurts you (or the ones you love) can expect no mercy from you. You can forget, but it's impossible to forgive.

However, it's a real privilege to be allowed into your inner circle. You are caring and devoted, and feel most at home in a warm, safe group environment. Feeling safe and secure is vitally important to you, because you're incredibly sensitive, so your emotions may fluctuate wildly sometimes. You are strongly family-oriented and tend to pull your friends into a close-knit family structure. The cringeworthy word 'framily' was invented just for you. What you seek in a partner is someone who can offer you emotional stability, while you mother them. Make sure that doesn't get out of hand.

LEO

When you walk into a room, tables are cleared and spotlights are swivelled, because everyone knows that you're about to claim the stage – improvised or otherwise. You love being the centre of attention; you always seek the spotlight and squeeze one more decibel out of your voice, so you'll soar above the rest. It's not horrible, but no one wants to sing a duet with you in karaoke.

You are proud and egocentric, but your warm personality, enthusiasm, can-do attitude, and ability to always see the positive in anyone or anything make people want to be around you, even if it's just to bask in the glow of your light.

When your moon in Leo is combined with your sun in a calmer sign of the zodiac, it may cause an internal conflict. Deep inside, you want that attention and don't feel validated unless you get it, but you may not always demand attention in the right ways. That causes friction which gets in your way more than anybody else's, and may cause you to come across as a bit bitter, petty and bossy as you channel your frustrations.

Generally, however, you are passionate and generous. You are looking for a partner who puts you on a pedestal, but give much of yourself in return – so much, in fact, that people sometimes venture to make a profit off you.

VIRGO

COMPATIBLE WITH
Taurus
Capricorn
Cancer

CLASHES WITH
Aries
Gemini
Leo

**FAMOUS PEOPLE
WITH THE SAME
MOON SIGN**
Stephen Hawking
Jodie Foster
Samuel L. Jackson
Madonna
Serena Williams

If there are any stray typos in this book that slipped past the proofreaders, you spotted them immediately. People with their sun or moon in Virgo are incredibly meticulous and perfectionist with a keen eye for detail. In fact, Virgos are so detail-oriented that we refuse to let any surgeons operate on us if they don't share the same zodiac sign. If you're more likely to sing the praises of others, that's fine too – even if it is a waste of your talent.

Still, your career probably hasn't led you down that path. You aren't all that interested in being the centre of attention; you're more likely to be quiet and reserved. People who don't know you well may think you're a bit of a cold fish – and honestly, people who do know you well might agree. You have some wonderful qualities, too: You are caring, devoted and helpful, especially when you can make yourself useful in practical ways. Homemade spaghetti sauce may be your love language. Household chores are bliss, and order and routine are the watchwords that you try to live by in every aspect of your life.

You need a partner who can handle your excessive concern and your periodic need for mental and physical space, but you also need someone who pulls you out of your comfort zone every now and then. A cartilage piercing in your tragus will heal exceptionally quickly, and help a lot with your tension headaches that you 'occasionally' seem to get.

LIBRA

Before you immediately glance down to see who you clash with: not everyone has to like you. In actual fact, at this very moment, you're probably Facebook friends with at least ten people who secretly can't stand you. And that's okay. It's a bitter pill to swallow, though, for a people-pleaser like you, who avoids stress and conflict at all costs. People with their moon in Libra are calm and loving, and will do anything they can to keep the peace. If everyone could just be like you, we would have achieved world peace a long time ago.

You do need a 'partner in peace', however, even if it's just so he or she can decide what you two will be having for dinner that night. In any case, you're the type who seems to glide effortlessly from one relationship into the next, a classic serial monogamist. Not that you let just anyone hold your hand, or other parts of your body. Your preference for beauty is not limited to an interest in art museums or a beautifully decorated living room. A sweetheart who isn't good-looking isn't an option for you.

Because the world is strange and wonderful, these people with their moon in Libra, who have a hard time making decisions and care a lot about external appearances, are likely to believe in true love despite it all.

Thanks, universe.

SCORPIO

COMPATIBLE WITH
Pisces
Leo
Cancer

CLASHES WITH
Aquarius
Gemini
Sagittarius

**FAMOUS PEOPLE
WITH THE SAME
MOON SIGN**
Katrin Swartenbroux
Mark Zuckerberg
Jules Verne
Beyoncé
Steven Spielberg
Lady Gaga

Scorpios are quite, how can we put it delicately, intense. You're all or nothing, equally capable of surrendering entirely to people or situations or walking away without a qualm. Spending time with you means stepping into the emotional rollercoaster that is your life, although you don't let people in easily. Your deepest, darkest thoughts remain private. At the same time, you're amazingly good at figuring other people out and surprising them with your accurate analysis at unexpected moments. It's not fair, Scorpio, but it is intriguing.

You invest 100% of yourself in whatever you do and expect people around you to do the same. You're not always conventional in your approach to relationships, but sincerity is vitally important to you; cowards and fakes need not apply. That's part of why you tend to be a bit suspicious, jealous and easily disappointed by life.

People with their moon in Scorpio want constant emotional and intellectual stimulus. You're not interested in small talk; instead, you see every conversation as an opportunity to establish a deep connection. As a passionate sign, sex is one of the ways that you pursue that connection. It's never boring with you, in any case, and you are open to every challenge. The best way to lure a Scorpio Moon out of his or her lair? Tell them 'bet you can't do it/don't have the guts'.

What you're holding right now is the result of a bet exactly like that.

SAGITTARIUS

Such a sweet summer child! People with their moon in Sagittarius are open, enthusiastic and friendly. They tend to be happy-go-lucky types that may earn tons of money working in hospitality because literally everyone wants to give them big tips, like the cabin crew member who keeps smiling even as the plane is crashing.

Your carefree nature may rub some people the wrong way, giving the impression of nonchalance. Rules and social conventions aren't really your thing in your job or in your relationships, whether romantic or just friendly. You're the friend who takes six days to respond to a text message, but then offers a very enthusiastic invitation to a party at your house.

The flipside of your spontaneous impulsiveness is that you're incredibly restless and quickly get tired of things or people. That can be confusing, since you throw yourself passionately into projects or relationships. Lots of people will find it difficult to stay on the same wavelength as you, without feeling hurt by your actions. You mean well, but you feel an intense need for freedom, personal space and variety. You absolutely love to travel, and there's a good chance that you are reading this book on the plane or sitting quietly by the seaside. Good for you, Sagittarius. But maybe you should text your mum?

CAPRICORN

Conscientious, ambitious and rational: those are your core qualities. You're at your best when you can be productive, work towards a purpose, and contribute to something bigger. Team-work makes the dream work and so on, but don't lose sight of who you are in the process. Capricorns are exceptionally hard on themselves and will always put goals before feelings.

You take a no-nonsense approach and have a strong sense of responsibility. Based on your attitude, people who don't know you might think you're arrogant, but you're actually just calm and a bit reserved and, sure, don't really have a fantastic sense of humour. Hopefully, you'll appreciate our efforts to keep this description as cut and dried as possible.

Power and status are very important to you, but you're not the type to hang around bars bragging loudly about the success of your latest ventures. You're very good at saving money, but investing in your personal life isn't your strongest suit.

Your partners often accuse you of being emotionally distant, because you are reserved about showing your emotions. When a friend or loved one tells you about a problem, you'll always start trying to figure out a solution for them, rather than offer-ing comfort. In fact, you may be uneasy when people openly show their emotions, whether they're feeling enthusiastic or sad. Your future spouse shouldn't expect you to be wiping away tears at weddings or funerals, but they can count on you to have everything arranged, down to the smallest detail.

AQUARIUS

COMPATIBLE WITH
Libra
Gemini
Leo

CLASHES WITH
Taurus
Cancer
Virgo

**FAMOUS PEOPLE
WITH THE SAME
MOON SIGN**
Orson Welles
Margaret Atwood
Angela Merkel
Britney Spears
Morgan Freeman

Kumbaya, dear Aquarius, kumbaya. You're a person who will sacrifice themselves for the greater good. You're the opposite of egocentric: as long as you can serve a higher purpose or have the idea you can make the world a better place, you're in your element. People whose moon is in Aquarius would do great in politics, but few of them, sadly, seek that calling.

Although you want to help 'the group' move forward, you're an independent person who prefers to retain your independence.

By definition, you're a social visionary; you may actually manage to make the world a better place because you're one of those rare individuals who is both analytical and creative, although possibly a bit eccentric. Your ideas are often so progressive, so far ahead of their time, but you always have to wait a decade before you can unleash a patient 'I told you so' on the world. You are open-minded and motivated, qualities that benefit your employer or your partner, as long as it's a good match.

As far as emotions go, you are cool but not closed off. It's easy for you to talk about your feelings and unconventional thoughts, but the problem is that the way you feel tends to change at times. You have a very wide-ranging circle of friends, and you tend to adapt to the overall tendencies of whichever group you're in at any given moment. But you won't find chameleon in the astrological bestiary of the zodiac.

PISCES

Sorry in advance, dear Pisces. We know that you're incredibly sensitive. You care deeply about everything, and your emotions are bigger than your body can contain, no matter how generously curvy your figure is. Life is hard, life is beautiful, life is ... abundant, possibly even too much, as you experience it. You're not just a whirlwind of emotions yourself, but you're also intensely empathetic, allowing you to be keenly aware of how others are feeling.

No, you're not exactly feeling like (sorry, couldn't resist) a fish in water as you move through life. Others don't understand how sensitive you are and how careful they need to be around you, which leads to frustrations; you may sometimes get wrapped up in feeling like a victim. Your oversensitivity mainly pays off for others: you are an amazingly sweet, generous, caring and loyal person who would drop everything to help someone. When you hurt someone, you tend to withdraw completely and go into a creative space.

Your astounding creativity is the advantage of being so highly sensitive. None of the other zodiac signs are more capable of understanding art, and creating it. People whose moon is in Pisces are frequently artists, poets or writers – or in some cases, as this book proves, all three.

ADDENDA

◖

Whether you're looking to schedule a steamy date or organise an artistic photo shoot, it can be useful to see at a glance when the moon will be smiling down on you. The following pages provide a lunar calendar and an overview of the lunar cycle for the next few years.

LUNAR PHASES 2020

● NEW MOON		◐ FIRST QUARTER		○ FULL MOON		◑ THIRD QUARTER	
		Jan. 3, Fri	05:46	Jan. 10, Fri	20:23	Jan. 17, Fri	14:00
Jan. 24, Fri	22:44	Feb. 2, Sun	02:43	Feb. 9, Sun	08:34	Feb. 15, Sat	23:19
Feb. 23, Sun	16:33	Mar. 2, Tue	20:58	Mar. 9, Mon	18:48	Mar. 16, Mon	10:35
Mar. 24, Tue	10:29	Apr. 1, Thu	12:21	Apr. 8, Wed	04:35	Apr. 15, Wed	00:56
Apr. 23, Thu	04:27	Apr. 30, Thu	22:38	May 7, Thu	12:45	May 14, Thu	16:03
May 22, Fri	19:39	May 30, Fri	05:30	June 5, Fri	21:12	June 13, Sat	08:24
June 21, Sun	08:42	June 28, Sun	10:16	July 5, Sun	06:44	July 13, Mon	01:31
July 20, Mon	19:33	July 27, Mon	14:33	Aug. 3, Mon	17:59	Aug. 11, Tue	18:47
Aug. 19, Wed	04:42	Aug. 25, Wed	19:59	Sept. 2, Wed	07:23	Sept. 10, Thu	11:28
Sept. 17, Thu	13:00	Sept. 24, Thu	03:56	Oct. 1, Thu	23:06	Oct. 10, Sat	02:41
Oct. 16, Fri	21:32	Oct. 23, Fri	15:24	Oct. 31, Sat	15:51	Nov. 8, Sun	14:47
Nov. 15, Sun	06:08	Nov. 22, Sun	05:45	Nov. 30, Mon	10:32	Dec. 8, Tue	01:37
Dec. 14, Mon	17:18	Dec. 22, Mon	00:42	Dec. 30, Wed	04:30		

LUNAR PHASES 2021

● NEW MOON		◐ FIRST QUARTER		○ FULL MOON		◑ THIRD QUARTER	
						Jan. 6, Wed	10:38
Jan. 13, Wed	06:02	Jan. 20, Wed	22:03	Jan. 28, Thu	20:18	Feb. 4, Thu	18:38
Feb. 11, Thu	20:08	Feb. 19, Fri	19:49	Feb. 27, Sat	09:19	Mar. 6, Sat	02:32
Mar. 13, Sat	11:23	Mar. 21, Sun	15:41	Mar. 28, Sun	20:50	Apr. 4 Sun	12:04
Apr. 12, Mon	04:32	Apr. 20, Tue	09:00	Apr. 27, Tue	05:33	May 3, Mon	21:51
May 11, Tue	21:01	May 19, May	21:13	May 26, Wed	13:14	June 2, Wed	09:26
June 10, Thu	12:54	June 18, Fri	05:54	June 24, Thu	20:40	July 1, Thu	23:12
July 10, Sat	03:17	July 17, Sat	12:11	July 24, Sat	04:37	July 31, Sat	15:18
Aug. 8, Sun	15:50	Aug. 15, Sun	17:21	Aug. 22, Sun	14:02	Aug. 30, Mon	09:15
Sept. 7, Tue	02:52	Sept. 13, Mon	22:41	Sept. 21, Tue	01:54	Sept. 29, Wed	03:58
Oct. 6, Wed	13:05	Oct. 13, Wed	05:27	Oct. 20, Wed	16:57	Oct. 28, Thu	22:06
Nov. 4, Thu	22:15	Nov. 11, Thu	13:48	Nov. 19, Fri	09:59	Nov. 27, Sat	13:29
Dec. 4, Sat	08:44	Dec. 11, Sat	02:37	Dec. 19, Sun	05:37	Dec. 27, Mon	03:26

LUNAR PHASES 2022

● NEW MOON		◐ FIRST QUARTER		○ FULL MOON		◑ THIRD QUARTER	
Jan. 2, Sun	19:35	Jan. 9, Sun	19:13	Jan. 18, Tue	00:51	Jan. 25, Tue	14:42
Feb. 1, Tue	06:49	Feb. 9, Tue	14:51	Feb. 16, Wed	17:59	Feb. 23, Wed	23:34
Mar. 2, Wed	18:38	Mar. 10, Don	11:46	Mar. 18, Fri	08:20	Mar. 25, Fri	06:39
Apr. 1, Fri	08:27	Apr. 9, Sat	08:48	Apr. 16, Sat	20:57	Apr. 23, Sat	13:58
Apr. 30, Sat	22:30	May 9, Mon	02:22	May 16, Mon	06:15	May 22, Sun	20:44
May 30, Mon	13:32	June 7, Tue	16:49	June 14, Tue	13:52	June 21, Tue	05:11
June 29, Wed	04:53	July 7, Don	04:14	July 13, Wed	20:38	July 20, Wed	16:19
July 28, Don	19:55	Aug. 5, Fri	13:07	Aug. 12, Fri	03:36	Aug. 19, Fri	06:36
Aug. 27, Sat	10:16	Sept. 3, Sat	20:08	Sept. 10, Sat	11:58	Sept. 17, Sat	23:52
Sept. 25, Sun	23:54	Oct. 3, Mon	02:15	Oct. 9, Sun	22:54	Oct. 17, Mon	19:16
Oct. 25, Tue	12:48	Nov. 1, Tue	07:38	Nov. 8, Tue	12:02	Nov. 16, Wed	14:29
Nov. 23, Wed	23:57	Nov. 30, Wed	15:38	Dec. 8, Don	05:09	Dec. 16, Fri	09:59
Dec. 23, Fri	11:17	Dec. 30, Fri	02:22				

LUNAR PHASES 2023

● NEW MOON		◐ FIRST QUARTER		○ FULL MOON		◑ THIRD QUARTER	
				Jan. 7, Sat	00:09	Jan. 15, Sun	03:13
Jan. 21, Sat	21:55	Jan. 28, Sat	02:43	Feb. 5, Sun	19:30	Feb. 13, Mon	17:03
Feb. 20, Mon	08:09	Feb. 23, Sun	20:58	Mar. 7, Tue	13:42	Mar. 15, Wed	03:10
Mar. 21, Tue	18:26	Mon. 24, Tue	12:21	Apr. 6, Thu	06:37	Apr. 13, Thu	11:12
Apr. 20, Thu	06:15	Apr. 23, Thu	22:38	May 5, Fri	19:36	May 12, Fri	16:29
May 19, Fri	17:55	May 22, Fri	05:30	June 4, Sun	05:43	June 10, Sat	21:32
June 18, Sun	06:39	June 21, Sun	10:16	July 3, Mon	13:40	July 10, Mon	03:49
July 17, Mon	20:33	July 20, Mon	14:33	Aug. 1, Tue	20:33	Aug. 8, Tue	12:29
Aug. 16, Wed	11:38	Aug. 19, Wed	19:59	Aug. 31, Thu	03:37	Sept. 7, Thu	00:22
Sept. 15, Fri	03:40	Sept. 17, Thu	03:56	Sept. 29, Fri	11:58	Oct. 6, Fri	15:49
Oct. 14, Sat	19:55	Oct. 16, Fri	15:24	Oct. 28, Sat	22:24	Nov. 5, Sun	09:38
Nov. 13, Mon	10:27	Nov. 15, Sun	05:45	Nov. 27, Mon	10:16	Dec. 58, Tue	06:51
Dec. 13, Wed	00:32	Dec. 14, Mon	00:42	Dec. 27, Wed	01:33		

LUNAR PHASES 2024

● NEW MOON		◑ FIRST QUARTER		○ FULL MOON		◐ THIRD QUARTER	
						Jan. 4, Thu	04:32
Jan. 11, Thu	12:58	Jan. 18, Thu	04:53	Jan. 25, Thu	18:54	Feb. 3, Sat	00:20
Feb. 10, Sat	00:00	Feb. 16, Fri	16:02	Feb. 24, Sat	13:31	Mar. 3, Sun	16:25
Mar. 10, Sun	10:02	Mar. 17, Sun	05:11	Mar. 25, Mon	08:01	Apr. 2, Tue	05:15
Apr. 8, Mon	20:23	Apr. 15, Mon	21:14	Apr. 24, Wed	01:51	May 1, Wed	13:27
May 8, Wed	05:24	May 15, Wed	13:49	May 23, Thu	15:55	May 30, Thu	19:13
June 6, Thu	14:40	June 14, Fri	07:19	June 22, Sat	03:10	June 28, Fri	23:55
July 6, Sat	00:59	July 14, Sun	00:49	July 21, Sun	12:19	July 28, Sun	04:54
Aug. 4, Sun	13:14	Aug. 12, Mon	17:19	Aug. 19, Mon	20:28	Aug. 26, Mon	11:28
Sept. 3, Tue	03:56	Sept. 11, Wed	08:06	Sept. 18, Wed	04:36	Sept. 24, Tue	20:52
Oct. 2, Wed	20:50	Oct. 10, Thu	20:56	Oct. 17, Thu	13:27	Oct. 24, Thu	10:05
Nov. 1, Fri	13:48	Nov. 9, Sat	06:56	Nov. 15, Fri	22:29	Nov. 23, Sat	02:29
Dec. 1, Sun	07:22	Dec. 8, Sun	16:27	Dec. 15, Sun	10:02	Dec. 22, Sun	23:19
Dec. 31, Mon	23:27						

LUNAR PHASES 2025

● NEW MOON		◑ FIRST QUARTER		○ FULL MOON		◐ THIRD QUARTER	
		Jan. 7, Tue	00:57	Jan. 13, Mon	23:27	Jan. 21, Tue	14:00
Jan. 29, Wed	13:37	Feb. 5, Wed	09:03	Feb. 12, Wed	14:54	Feb. 20, Thu	23:19
Feb. 28, Fri	01:46	Mar. 6, Thu	17:33	Mar. 14, Fri	07:55	Mar. 22, Sat	10:35
Mar. 29, Sat	12:00	Apr. 5, Sat	04:16	Apr. 13, Sun	02:23	Apr. 21, Mon	00:56
Apr. 27, Sun	21:33	May 4, Sun	15:53	May 12, Mon	18:58	May 20, Tue	16:03
May 27, Tue	05:04	June 3, Tue	05:41	June 11, Wed	09:46	June 18, Wed	08:24
June 25, Wed	12:33	July 2, Wed	21:30	July 10, Thu	22:38	July 18, Fri	01:31
July 24, Thu	21:12	Aug. 1, Fri	14:41	Aug. 9, Sat	09:57	Aug. 16, Sat	18:47
Aug. 23, Sat	08:07	Aug. 31, Sun	08:25	Sept. 7, Sun	20:10	Sept. 14, Sun	11:28
Sept. 21, Sun	21:54	Sept. 30, Tue	01:54	Oct. 7, Tue	05:48	Oct. 13, Mon	02:41
Oct. 21, Tue	14:25	Oct. 29, Wed	17:22	Nov. 5, Wed	14:20	Nov. 12, Wed	14:47
Nov. 20, Thu	07:48	Nov. 28, Fri	07:59	Dec. 8, Fri	00:15	Dec. 11, Thu	01:37
Dec. 20, Sat	02:44	Dec. 27, Sat	20:10				

MOON CALENDAR 2020

	JAN	FEB	MAR	APR	MAY	JUN	JUL	AUG	SEP	OCT	NOV	DEC	
1													1
2													2
3													3
4													4
5													5
6													6
7													7
8													8
9													9
10													10
11													11
12													12
13													13
14													14
15													15
16													16
17													17
18													18
19													19
20													20
21													21
22													22
23													23
24													24
25													25
26													26
27													27
28													28
29													29
30													30
31													31

MOON CALENDAR 2021

	JAN	FEB	MAR	APR	MAY	JUN	JUL	AUG	SEP	OCT	NOV	DEC	
1													1
2													2
3													3
4													4
5													5
6													6
7													7
8													8
9													9
10													10
11													11
12													12
13													13
14													14
15													15
16													16
17													17
18													18
19													19
20													20
21													21
22													22
23													23
24													24
25													25
26													26
27													27
28													28
29													29
30													30
31													31

181

MOON CALENDAR 2022

	JAN	FEB	MAR	APR	MAY	JUN	JUL	AUG	SEP	OCT	NOV	DEC	
1													1
2													2
3													3
4													4
5													5
6													6
7													7
8													8
9													9
10													10
11													11
12													12
13													13
14													14
15													15
16													16
17													17
18													18
19													19
20													20
21													21
22													22
23													23
24													24
25													25
26													26
27													27
28													28
29													29
30													30
31													31

MOON CALENDAR 2023

	JAN	FEB	MAR	APR	MAY	JUN	JUL	AUG	SEP	OCT	NOV	DEC	
1	◐	◐	◐	◐	◐	○	○	○	○	○	○	○	1
2	◐	○	◐	◐	◐	○	○	○	○	○	○	○	2
3	○	○	◐	◐	◐	○	○	○	○	○	○	○	3
4	○	○	○	○	○	○	○	○	◑	◑	◑	◑	4
5	○	○	○	○	○	○	○	◑	◑	◑	◑	◑	5
6	○	○	○	○	○	○	○	◑	◑	◑	◑	◑	6
7	○	○	○	○	○	○	◑	◑	◑	●	●	●	7
8	○	○	○	○	○	◑	◑	◑	●	●	●	●	8
9	◑	○	○	○	◑	◑	◑	◑	●	●	●	●	9
10	◑	○	○	○	◑	◑	◑	●	●	●	●	●	10
11	◑	◑	○	◑	◑	◑	◑	●	●	●	●	●	11
12	◑	◑	◑	◑	◑	●	●	●	●	●	●	●	12
13	◑	◑	◑	◑	●	●	●	●	●	●	●	●	13
14	◑	◑	◑	●	●	●	●	●	●	●	●	●	14
15	◑	●	◑	●	●	●	●	●	●	●	●	●	15
16	◑	●	●	●	●	●	●	●	●	●	●	◐	16
17	◑	●	●	●	●	●	●	●	●	●	◐	◐	17
18	●	●	●	●	●	●	●	●	◐	◐	◐	◐	18
19	●	●	●	●	●	●	●	◐	◐	◐	◐	◐	19
20	●	●	●	●	●	●	◐	◐	◐	◐	◐	◐	20
21	●	●	●	●	●	◐	◐	◐	◐	◐	○	◐	21
22	●	●	●	●	◐	◐	◐	◐	◐	◐	○	○	22
23	●	●	●	◐	◐	◐	◐	◐	○	○	○	○	23
24	●	●	◐	◐	◐	◐	◐	○	○	○	○	○	24
25	●	◐	◐	◐	◐	◐	○	○	○	○	○	○	25
26	◐	◐	◐	◐	◐	○	○	○	○	○	○	○	26
27	◐	◐	◐	◐	○	○	○	○	○	○	○	○	27
28	◐	◐	◐	◐	○	○	○	○	○	○	○	○	28
29	◐		◐	◐	◐	○	○	○	○	○	○	○	29
30	◐		◐	◐	◐	○	○	○	○	○	○	○	30
31	◐		◐		◐		○	○		○		○	31

MOON CALENDAR 2024

	JAN	FEB	MAR	APR	MAY	JUN	JUL	AUG	SEP	OCT	NOV	DEC	
1													1
2													2
3													3
4													4
5													5
6													6
7													7
8													8
9													9
10													10
11													11
12													12
13													13
14													14
15													15
16													16
17													17
18													18
19													19
20													20
21													21
22													22
23													23
24													24
25													25
26													26
27													27
28													28
29													29
30													30
31													31

MOON CALENDAR 2025

	JAN	FEB	MAR	APR	MAY	JUN	JUL	AUG	SEP	OCT	NOV	DEC	
1													1
2													2
3													3
4													4
5													5
6													6
7													7
8													8
9													9
10													10
11													11
12													12
13													13
14													14
15													15
16													16
17													17
18													18
19													19
20													20
21													21
22													22
23													23
24													24
25													25
26													26
27													27
28													28
29													29
30													30
31													31

A designated Dark Sky Park preserves the best and brightest starry skies by protecting the nights from local artificial lighting. Here's an overview of the designated parks at the end of 2019, but the plan is to keep expanding the list every year in the fight against encroaching light pollution.

A

uan Mountain, TAIWAN
ote-Ishigaki National Park, JAPAN
on Crater, ISRAEL
gyang Firefly Eco Park, SOUTH KOREA

OPE

nyà, SPAIN
rcroy National Park and Wild Nephin Wilderness, IRELAND
min Moor Dark Sky Landscape, ENGLAND
National Park, HUNGARY
oschplaat, THE NETHERLANDS
National Park, GERMANY
Valley Estate, WALES
way Forest Park, SCOTLAND
obágy National Park, HUNGARY
versmeer National Park, THE NETHERLANDS
and Nyord, DENMARK
humberland National Park and Kielder Water
    and Forest Park, ENGLAND
va gora-Biljeg, CROATIA
ntoul and Glenlivet – Cairngorms, SCOTLAND
lmoosalm, GERMANY
c National Landscape Protection Area, HUNGARY

TH AMERICA

lope Island State Park, USA
-Borrego Desert State Park, USA
ypress National Preserve, USA
Canyon of the Gunnison National Park, USA
e Canyon National Park, USA
lo National River, USA
onlands National Park, USA
tol Reef National Park, USA
lin Volcano National Monument, USA
ar Breaks National Monument, USA
o Culture National Historical Park, USA
ry Springs State Park, USA
ton Lake State Park, USA
er Breaks State Park, USA
ers of the Moon National Monument, USA
Horse Point State Park, USA
h Valley National Park, USA
saur National Monument, USA
anted Rock State Natural Area, USA
Union National Monument, USA

Geauga Observatory Park, USA
Goblin Valley State Park, USA
Grand Canyon National Park, USA
Grand Canyon–Parashant National Monument, USA
Great Basin National Park, USA
Great Sand Dunes National Park and Preserve, USA
Headlands, USA
Hovenweep National Monument, USA
James River State Park, USA
Joshua Tree National Park, USA
Kartchner Caverns State Park, USA
Kissimmee Prairie Preserve State Park, USA
Mayland Earth to Sky Park and Bare Dark Sky
    Observatory, USA
Middle Fork River Forest Preserve, USA
Natural Bridges National Monument, USA
Newport State Park, USA
Obed Wild and Scenic River, USA
Oracle State Park, USA
Petrified Forest National Park, USA
Pickett CCC Memorial State Park and Pogue Creek
    Canyon State Natural Area, USA
Rappahannock County Park, USA
Salinas Pueblo Missions National Monument, USA
South Llano River State Park, USA
Staunton River State Park, USA
Steinaker State Park, USA
Stephen C. Foster State Park, USA
Tonto National Monument, USA
Tumacácori National Historical Park, USA
UBarU Camp and Retreat Center, USA
Waterton-Glacier International Peace Park,
    CANADA AND USA
Weber County North Fork Park, USA

OCEANIA

Warrumbungle National Park, AUSTRALIA

Astrology is an ancient practice that can be complicated to comprehend on your own. These apps, podcasts and Instagram accounts offer deeper insights, practical updates and surprising applications so you won't need to generate and analyse your star chart every day. Quite convenient!

APPS

MOON PHASE

app gives you a lunar calendar on your phone. It provides
mation on the current lunar phase and when the moon will
and set, and gives easy options for looking up when the
full moon will be. Fun extra feature: the app also shows you
n the 'golden' and 'blue' hours of the moon will be, so you can
edule your lunar snapshots exactly the way you want them.
able for iOS and Android

STAR ASTROLOGY

ultimate astrology app. Co-Star calculates your birth chart
you, so you'll know exactly where the planets were when
were born and how that affects your personality. You get a
iled daily horoscope which is often frighteningly accurate,
the position of the various planets in your chart clearly
ws how long a difficult emotional period will last for you. If
friends install the app, you can link your profiles and see
re you're astrologically matched and where you clash –
t for first dates. The app's sleek design and daily updates
a funny twist (almost impossible not to share!) are very
ealing. *available for iOS*

VIEW APP

tronomy is the main reason for your interest in the moon (and
ything surrounding it), then SkyView will be very interesting.
starwatching app uses your camera and your location data
earch for and identify the constellations in the night sky. The
provides a very accessible way to learn more about star
ems, galaxies, and the satellites orbiting above you, and you
locate all the constellations and familiar stars in the heavens.
lable for iOS and Android

TIME PASSAGES

An astrology app that provides information on the positions
of the planets and how they affect you and everyone around
you – much like Co-Star. For an additional 99 cents, you also
get a detailed birth chart, although Co-Star is a little clearer in
explaining what it means. The nice thing about Time Passages is
that the app gives a very good explanation of what all the planets
mean, so it teaches you to understand and read astrology better
on your own. Also fun: the app lets you look up celebrities to see
what their birth chart looks like, what kind of personality they
have, and whether or not you would be a good match. *available
for iOS and Android*

MY MOONTIME

This fertility and menstruation tracker shows the moon's
influence on a woman's monthly cycle and shows you your most
fertile days. The app also offers convenient information on mood
swings, pregnancy and menopause.

PODCASTS

13 MINUTES TO THE MOON
A short but fun podcast about the moon landing, the incredible tale of Apollo 11 and how it almost went wrong, and what that one small step truly meant to mankind.

NASA EXPLORERS:
APOLLO & HOUSTON, WE HAVE A PODCAST
NASA releases excellent podcasts, filled with interviews featuring experts, technical specialists and astronauts, supplemented by archival material and exclusive behind-the-scenes audio clips. These two podcasts are just a small sample of the extensive array available on the NASA website.

CONVERSATIONS WITH MOON BODY SOUL
Talks to inspire and intrigue you, giving more insight and fresh energy. Kaitee Tyner, founder of self-care company Moon Body Soul, features a different guest on each episode.

ASTROPOETS
A unique combination of astrology, spoken word, poetry, internet culture and humour from astrologists Dorothea Lasky and Alex Dimitrov, whose keen observations and funny memes have also been very successful on Twitter.

MUST-FOLLOW INSTAGRAM ACCOUNTS

@moonsistersmooncalendar

@moonomens

@moonlightenergyhealing

@current_moon_phase

@girlandhermoon

@moonbodysoul

@themoon_journal

@chaninicholas

@the.moon.calendar

@mysticmama

@thehoodwitch

@spiritdaughter

@risingwoman

@thefieldwork

@lanabauwens

@maximevossen

@the_moondeck

@Gottess

@Mylkymoonlab

@Dreamymoon

COLOPHON

PHOTOCREDITS

This book is MARKED

MARKED is an initiative by Lannoo Publishers.
www.markedbooks.be

JOIN THE MARKED COMMUNITY on @markedbylannoo

Or sign up for our MARKED newsletter with news about new and forthcoming publications on art, interior design, food & travel, photography and fashion as well as exclusive offers and MARKED events on www.markedbooks.be

TEXTS
Wided Bouchrika
Katrin Swartenbroux

TRANSLATION
Joy Phillips

COPY-EDITING
Lisa Holden

BOOK DESIGN
Lisbeth Antoine

TYPESETTING
Lisbeth Antoine and Keppie & Keppie

If you have any questions or comments about the material in this book, please do not hesitate to contact our editorial team: markedteam@lannoo.com.

D/2020/45/44 - NUR 450/882
ISBN: 9789401465700
www.lannoo.com

5 *Paint It Black*, © Sammy Slabbinck / **8** © NASA / **12** © i͏ **14** © The Wellcome Collection / **16** © The Wellcome Colle **18** © NASA / **21** (above and middle) © Imageselect (below) © NASA / **22** Man on the Moon, © Sammy Slabbi **23** *Bath Time*, © Sammy Slabbinck / **25** © NASA / **30** © S Zabelina, fotografie: Maro Hagopian / **33** © Myriam Ach Soumati Studio/ **34** © Joke De Coninck / **36** © My Achour - Soumati Studio/ **39-40** © Kim Hertogs - Fieldwork, fotografie: Wouter Struyf / **44-45** © Imagese **46** *Moonwalk 405 (Pink)*, Andy Warhol © Imageselect *Eclips*, © Sammy Slabbinck / **54** © ZUMA press / **59** © Center for British Art, Paul Mellon Collection / **61** © Im select / **67** © Holly Stapleton / **68** © Holly Stapleton (below) © Metropolitan Museum of Modern Art / **74** (a⊩ © The National Gallery, London (below) © Imageselect (above and below) © Imageselect / **79** (above and b⊩ © Imageselect / **80** (above and below) © Imageselect (above and below) © Imageselect / **84** (above) © Pau Hoeydonck (below) © Cristina de Middel/Magnum Phc **89** © Imageselect / **92** © NASA / **100** © Leen De Ridder *Brassaï's Moon. Journey of the Private Moon in Paris. Fr 2009*, Leonid Tishkov © Leonid Tishkov / **104** © iSt⊂ **108** *Moonlit Night on the Dnieper*, Arkhip Kuindzhi, © Im select / **111** *A Moonlit Lake by a Castle Joseph Wright of D* © Imageselect / **113** *Moon rise above the Syr Dary* © NASA / **114** © iStock / **117** © Imageselect / **131** © My Achour - Soumati Studio/ **133** © Lisbeth Antoine / **135** © Im select / **139** © Anabelle Ashley – Lunar Moon / **140** *d'étoiles*, Sophie Lécuyer / **146-147** *Goldmine in Λ Montana. Transylvania. Journey of the Private Moon in Rom 2015*, Leonid Tishkov © Leonid Tishkov / **149** © Imagesel **151** *Shelter. Qijin. Journey of the Private Moon on Taiwan,* Leonid Tishkov © Leonid Tishkov / **156** *Security Guard moon model in the Field Museum in Chicago*, © Imagese **161** 'Moon Gate 2' Mario Botta © Enrico Cano / **191** *Hou the Moon. On the pigeonry. Meinong. Journey of the P Moon on Taiwan, 2012*, Leonid Tishkov, © Leonid Tis